FLOYD CLYMER'S MOTORCYCLIST'S LIBRARY

The Book of the
HONDA TWINS

COVERING ALL TWIN-CYLINDER MODELS
UP TO 1968, EXCEPT THE 250 SUPER SPORTS

BY
JOHN THORPE

ANNOUNCEMENT

By special arrangement with the original publishers of this book, Sir Isaac Pitman & Son, Ltd., of London, England, we have secured the exclusive publishing rights for this book, as well as all others in THE MOTORCYCLIST'S LIBRARY.

Included in THE MOTORCYCLIST'S LIBRARY are complete instruction manuals covering the care and operation of respective motorcycles and engines; valuable data on speed tuning, and thrilling accounts of motorcycle race events. See listing of available titles elsewhere in this edition.

We consider it a privilege to be able to offer so many fine titles to our customers.

FLOYD CLYMER
Publisher of Books Pertaining to Automobiles and Motorcycles

2125 W. PICO ST.   LOS ANGELES 6, CALIF.

INTRODUCTION

Welcome to the world of digital publishing ~ the book you now hold in your hand, while unchanged from the original edition, was printed using the latest state of the art digital technology. The advent of print-on-demand has forever changed the publishing process, never has information been so accessible and it is our hope that this book serves your informational needs for years to come. If this is your first exposure to digital publishing, we hope that you are pleased with the results. Many more titles of interest to the classic automobile and motorcycle enthusiast, collector and restorer are available via our website at www.VelocePress.com. We hope that you find this title as interesting as we do.

NOTE FROM THE PUBLISHER

The information presented is true and complete to the best of our knowledge. All recommendations are made without any guarantees on the part of the author or the publisher, who also disclaim all liability incurred with the use of this information.

TRADEMARKS

We recognize that some words, model names and designations, for example, mentioned herein are the property of the trademark holder. We use them for identification purposes only. This is not an official publication.

INFORMATION ON THE USE OF THIS PUBLICATION

This manual is an invaluable resource for the classic motorcycle enthusiast and a "must have" for owners interested in performing their own maintenance. However, in today's information age we are constantly subject to changes in common practice, new technology, availability of improved materials and increased awareness of chemical toxicity. As such, it is advised that the user consult with an experienced professional prior to undertaking any procedure described herein. While every care has been taken to ensure correctness of information, it is obviously not possible to guarantee complete freedom from errors or omissions or to accept liability arising from such errors or omissions. Therefore, any individual that uses the information contained within, or elects to perform or participate in do-it-yourself repairs or modifications acknowledges that there is a risk factor involved and that the publisher or its associates cannot be held responsible for personal injury or property damage resulting from the use of the information or the outcome of such procedures.

WARNING!

One final word of advice, this publication is intended to be used as a reference guide, and when in doubt the reader should consult with a qualified technician.

Preface

My introduction to Hondas came at the Amsterdam Show of 1959 when, in common with a horde of other journalists, I joined the crush examining

Fig. 1. The 175 c.c. twin is one of the most popular Hondas ever to be produced. This is the U.K. version, without an electric starter. In some countries, however, a starter is used

the unfamiliar angularity of the first of the twins to be seen in Europe—a C.72.

At that time Japanese motor-cycles weren't so much a mystery as a

PREFACE

joke. The Japs, so we thought, were incapable of originating anything worthwhile. All they could do was copy. The joke was on us . . .

But, as I said, that was 1959. Times have changed—and in the decade that has followed I have not been alone in finding out that the Japanese in general, and Honda in particular, produce machines that are original from the word "go." And so far as Hondas are concerned that is a singularly appropriate word. They *do* go. And they keep on going. That

Fig. 2. The mighty 450—a machine for the real enthusiast who appreciates high performance and superlative workmanship

applies as much today as it did to the C.92 which formed my personal transport in 1962, and the hairy (but so refined) CB.72 which replaced it.

In this book, I have dealt with all the twins so far introduced, with the exception of the CB.250 Super Sports which is reserved until a later edition. So, in these pages you will be able to find all you need to look after your C.92 or CB.92, your C.95 or CB.160, your CD.175, C.72 or 77, CB.72 or 77, or your road-eating CB.450. But there is one proviso. You *must* use this book in conjunction with the standard Owner's Handbook, for the obvious reason that it is impossible in a volume of this size to describe overhaul and trouble-shooting procedures *and* give detailed day-to-day maintenance instructions for ten different motor-cycles. *Something* has had to go—and that something has been the elementary stuff which every rider worth his salt either knows by heart or can find out

PREFACE

from his Handbook. I have set out to supplement this and to go more deeply into the care of these fine machines.

In this, I have been helped considerably by Honda (U.K.) Ltd., who have supplied me with copious workshop manuals (which, alas, would all too frequently have been more intelligible had they been left in the original Japanese) and have readily allowed me to raid them for illustrations. This continues the close and courteous relationship I have enjoyed with the British branch of Honda ever since its foundation, and I am happy to record my debt to them once again.

BRIGHTON
SUSSEX

JOHN THORPE

PUBLISHER'S NOTE

Please note that the author states that this publication should be used "in conjunction with the standard Owner's Handbook". If you are seeking more comprehensive information we would recommend the following re-prints of the factory manuals that are also available from www.VelocePress.com.

HONDA MOTORCYCLES 125-150 TWINS C/CS/CB/CA FACTORY MANUAL: Applicable to the 125-150 series C92, CS92, CB92, C95 & CA95.

HONDA MOTORCYCLES 250-305 TWINS C/CS/CB FACTORY MANUAL: Applicable to the 250-305 series C72, C77, CS72, CS77, CB72, CB77 (Hawk).

VelocePress.com re-prints of additional Honda factory manuals include:

HONDA MOTORCYCLES C100 SUPER CUB FACTORY MANUAL
HONDA MOTORCYCLES C110 SPORT CUB 1962-1969 FACTORY MANUAL

Finally, for those enthusiasts that appreciate all Honda motorcycle products we also have the following publications available:

HONDA 50 ALL MODELS UP TO 1970 INC MONKEY & TRAIL (BOOK OF): Applicable to the C100, C102, C110, C114, C50, P50, PC50, PF50 OHV & PF50, and all 50cc Mini Trail and Monkey Bike variants.

HONDA 90 ALL MODELS UP TO 1966 (BOOK OF): Applicable to all 90cc variations including the S90, CM90, C200, S65, Trail 90 & C65 models.

HONDA TWINS & SINGLES 50cc TO 305cc 1960-1966 (BOOK OF): Applicable to the 50cc models C100, C102, Monkey Bike, CE105H Trails Bike, C110 & C114. The 125cc models C92, CB92 & Benley. The 250cc models C72 & CB72. The 305cc models C77, CB77.

Contents

Chapter	page
1. Method in your Maintenance	1
2. Tools for the Job	7
3. Looking After your Honda	11
4. Be your own Doctor	21
5. Trouble Tracing the Easy Way	29
6. Doing a Decoke	35
7. Working on the C. 92 and CB. 92	39
8. Working on the 160 c.c. unit	46
9. Working on the 175 c.c. unit	53
10. Working on the 250/305 c.c. units	58
11. Working on the 450 c.c. unit	64
12. Honda Carburettors	73
13. Suspension and Brakes	80
APPENDIX: Facts and Figures	86
Index	97

1 Method in your Maintenance

JUST as in everyday life it is more important to keep fit than to be forever undergoing medical treatment and major surgery, so with your Honda you should aim to keep it in good running order by constant attention to its everyday needs, and not let faults develop to the point where components need to be stripped and rebuilt.

Now this may seem obvious enough, on the face of it, yet there are far too many owners who do just the opposite. Their machines are constantly in pieces; yet small defects, neglected, are allowed to become major ones calling for a fresh strip-down to rectify the damage. The strip-down in turn disturbs parts which had already bedded in, and the efficiency of the entire machine suffers as a result.

Given the specified regular maintenance, any of the Honda models can cover quite a surprising mileage before there is any real need to strip the power unit or even—thanks to its own efficiency and to the additives in modern oils and fuels—to lift the head for a decoke. But if routine maintenance is neglected the time which can elapse between overhauls is shortened drastically—and so, too, is the life of the machine. To make matters worse the overhaul, when it comes, has to be more extensive (and more expensive) as a result.

The reason is simple—maladjustments have a cumulative effect. The Honda engines are tough—remarkably tough—but they are as much pieces of precision engineering as any watch. Like a top-quality watch, the Honda depends upon its precision for its performance, and faults which are allowed to develop will naturally throw it out of its stride. Take, for instance, a tight tappet. This will cause little enough harm if it is rectified within say, fifty miles. But in the absence of a routine check on tappet settings it could be left uncorrected for hundreds, or even thousands, of miles. Then all sorts of trouble can result from this one minor case of neglect. Searing hot gases from the combustion chamber—they reach temperatures of over 600°F—can play on the seating of the valve and on the valve stem like a blowtorch. Tough though they are, they will not withstand this treatment indefinitely, and eventually some of the metal is burned away. That leaves deep pits which, in turn, cut the compression still further, making the speed and acceleration drop off while fuel consumption rises. The entire engine is made to work harder to overcome this deficiency, wear is increased, and the life of such components as the pistons and the big-end and small-end bearings is reduced. Eventually, the least work which will make good the damage is to lift the head, recut the seat, and fit a new valve. Even assuming that there are no long-term effects, that's a pretty high price to pay for the couple of minutes saved by neglecting a weekly tappet check.

It is not, of course, only engines that can suffer in this way. The brakes are an equally glaring example. The linings wear slowly but constantly. The rider consequently gets used to their decreasing power, until the day arrives when he needs to stop in a hurry. Then he finds to his horror that they are not what they used to be, and he learns a hard lesson the dangerous way. Again, a constant routine check on brake

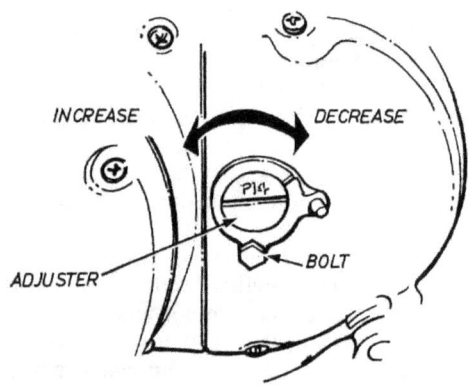

Fig. 3. This type of clutch adjustment is used on Honda twins to increase or decrease clearance. The lock-bolt must be loosened before the adjuster will turn. Tighten the bolt afterwards to hold the setting

adjustment—it takes a couple of minutes—will ensure that such a situation never arises.

Or, take the transmission. Out of sight inside its case, the chain is easily overlooked. Yet it has a big job to do and, inevitably, it wears. If it is not adjusted there is a danger that under certain conditions it could even jump off the sprocket and jam the rear wheel. And it will certainly damage the sprocket if it is allowed to run slack, because the power is then applied at the ends of the teeth, which eventually become hook-shaped. When that happens the sprocket and the chain both have to be replaced, because a hooked sprocket will ruin a new chain within a few hundred miles.

Normally, it is recommended that checks should be carried out on specified components at intervals of so many hundreds or thousands of miles. Providing you keep a detailed log book this is as good a way as any—but how many of us do? Can you say for certain at what mileage you last tensioned the chain? Or took up slack in the brakes? Or did

METHOD IN YOUR MAINTENANCE

any of the numerous jobs which the machine demands? I couldn't—not on that basis.

But then I use a different method—based on the "Task Systems" which were employed to keep military vehicles in order. The Automobile Association uses just such a scheme to get 100,000 miles or more from its patrol Minivans. It works! Set tasks are done each day, so that each week every essential job on the vehicle has been done and every vital

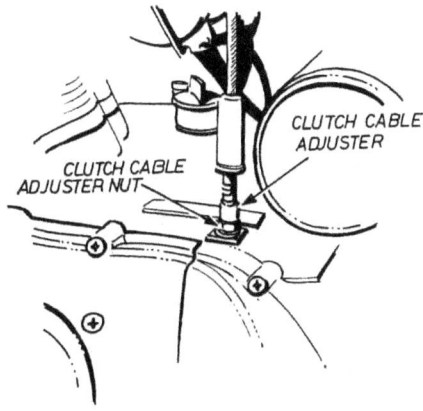

Fig. 4. This adjuster on the clutch cable gives a ready means of altering the clutch setting for minor adjustments only. Loosen the lock-nut before turning the adjuster, and tighten it afterwards

point checked. For your Honda, which does not—I hope—lead as hectic a life as the average Service or A.A. vehicle, the routine involved need not be exacting. One can work either to a daily or to a weekly system, depending on the machine's utilization. If it is in use every day the daily system, of course, is the more appropriate. Where it is used mainly at weekends the weekly system will prove adequate. Carrying out the recommended checks should involve, at worst, no more than 10 minutes' work each day and in most cases only a couple of minutes will be needed, for the idea is simply to check whether or not anything needs to be done. If the adjustment is already correct there is no need to touch it.

DAILY CHECK SYSTEM

Sunday. Check adjustment of front and rear brakes; check freedom of action of brake controls; check security of all nuts and bolts in the braking system; check lubrication of the brake cables and linkages.

Monday. Check engine/gearbox oil level; check final drive chain tension.

Tuesday. Examine all exposed electrical wiring for abrasion or fracture; test terminals for tightness; test all lamps and switchgear; check battery electrolyte level.

Wednesday. Examine tyre treads and remove any trapped stones; check tyre pressures; check spokes for security; rock wheels and fork to check wheel, head and pivot bearings.

Thursday. Check clutch adjustment.

Friday. Test all nuts and bolts for security; check operation of throttle and choke controls; check fuel flow through pipe.

Saturday. Check tappet settings; check sparking plugs for gap and condition; check contact-breaker points gap and condition.

ALTERNATIVE WEEKLY CHECK SYSTEM

Week 1. Check engine/gearbox oil levels; check tappet settings; check sparking plug gaps and plug condition; check contact-breaker for gap and condition of the points.

Week 2. Check the brakes for adjustment; check all controls for freedom of action and for lubrication; check wheels for loose spokes; test play in wheel, pivot and head bearings; examine tyre treads; test tyre pressures; check rear chain adjustment.

Week 3. Examine all electric wiring for fractures or abrasions; test terminals for security; check operation of lamps, horn and switchgear; check battery electrolyte level.

Week 4. Test clutch for adjustment; check fuel flow through pipe; test all nuts and bolts for security.

Whichever of these two systems you adopt, you will be certain that all major points will be checked at least once every month. Even allowing for a pretty substantial utilization of your Honda, that means that no more than 800 miles is likely to elapse between checks—and that most defects will be noted and rectified before they have had any chance to develop into serious faults.

Neither system, of course, covers such points as oil changes and greasing. These must still be carried out on an elapsed-mileage basis, since lubricant is exhausted through utilization, not by mere time. But here again you can guard against essential work being overlooked by sticking a piece of coloured tape on the machine and noting on the tape the mileage at which the next oil change and the next thorough greasing has to be done. Fix this tape somewhere you are bound to see it—inside the tool compartment or battery box, for instance.

It is a great mistake to overlook this periodic lubrication and, particularly, the oil changes. The Honda has only a small-capacity sump which serves both the engine and the gearbox, and the unit is very high-revving. That means the oil has got to be clean if it is to do its man-sized job. If the thin film of lubricant between the working surfaces were to break down the amount of wear which could occur in a very short time would be incredible.

Additionally, of course, the oil becomes contaminated in use. Tiny pieces of metal are rubbed off the pistons and the bearings and the gears as they move. For every gallon of fuel burned in the combustion chamber rather more than a gallon of water is produced, and though most of this is expelled into the exhaust system with the gases, a proportion of it finds its

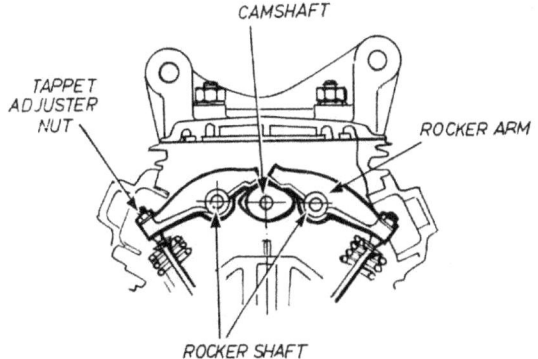

Fig. 5. A typical Honda single overhead camshaft layout applicable to all the twins except the double o.h.c. 450

way down the bore and into the sump. This is particularly so just after starting up, when the engine is cold and condensation occurs most readily. Once in the sump, the water mingles with the other products of combustion which manage to blow past the piston rings, and together they form sludge. Consequently, by the time the oil-change comes round that lubricant in the sump is no longer capable of doing its job properly.

It should be drained off when the engine is hot, so that it flows freely and carries with it as many impurities as possible. The drain plug should then be refitted and fresh oil of the correct grade used to replenish the sump. Don't use the wrong grade of oil. Before a grade is specified, technicians at the manufacturer's factory and in the laboratories of the oil companies carry out stringent tests to determine which is the best for any given unit. You cannot hope to better their choice; and in any case it is not worth risking a damaged engine or gearbox for the sake of saving a few pence on oil.

To ensure that the fresh oil is not contaminated with old oil, it is not at all a bad idea to give an intermediate flushing with a special flushing oil. This washes the oil passages clear. Then it is drained off—again, by removing both the oil filter cap and the drain plug, and the engine is allowed to stand for a quarter of an hour or so before the drain plug is replaced and the new lubricant poured in.

In all the engines dealt with in this book, the drain plug is located centrally, underneath the sump, and can be removed with a 17 mm spanner. All these models also have an oil filter—and some a gauze—which need to be cleaned. The filter is of centrifugal design, in which sludge and metallic particles are separated from the lubricant by the force of rotation. Instructions for dealing with the removal of the filter (and the oil strainer gauze, where appropriate) are given in the specialized chapters. These filters are cleaned by dismantling them and washing them thoroughly in petrol. After this has been done, it is essential to drain them and to allow any petrol residue to evaporate before refitting,

2 Tools for the Job

It is a ludicrous mistake to spend a couple of hundred pounds or more on a quality mount and then let it depreciate by grudging an extra expenditure of perhaps £5 on the tools which will keep it in good order. And the tool kit supplied with a Honda, even though it would put to shame those normally issued with most other makes, is really intended only for running repairs and general maintenance. For major work, it will pay to invest in a workshop kit which, over the years, will more than repay its initial cost. You will change your motor-cycle but your tool kit is there for good.

Specifically for the Honda, you will also need a certain number of special tools—a generator rotor puller, for example. Where such a tool is required, I have noted the fact in the text. Don't try to make do without it—Hondas are made to very fine limits indeed, and in these instances the special tool is designed to do a particular job without damaging the unit. It is no saving to keep a few shillings in your pocket by "improvising," when by doing so you may have halved the life of a component costing pounds to replace. So, if you haven't got the tool, don't do the job.

Spanners, screwdrivers and so forth are not special tools—but they are nonetheless essential ones. Buy the best that you can afford. Cheap tools are not really all that much cheaper, and they are neither as efficient nor as long-lasting. If you intend to become a real rider-mechanic (as most motor-cyclists do) get yourself some good chrome-vanadium spanners. A set of open-enders ranging from 8 mm to, say, 22 mm should be the first item on the list. Supplement this with a set of ring spanners—preferably from 6 mm upwards. And when you can really afford to go to town, get a socket set too. This cannot replace either the rings or the open-enders, but these tools are the most versatile of them all. You can obtain all manner of accessories to go with them—long and short extensions; an extension with universal joints so that you can operate round corners; ratchet wrenches which enable you to undo nuts with little more than flicks of the wrist; and a torque wrench which permits nuts and bolts to be tightened to an exact setting specified by the manufacturer.

If finances will not run to the socket set, you should at least obtain an assortment of stout box spanners and a really substantial tommy bar.

You will also need some additional screwdrivers. Excellent though the standard Honda screwdriver with its interchangeable blade is, my experience has been that it will not free really tight cross-headed screws. For this sort of job, the best answer is the workshop-type cross-headed screwdriver used by Honda mechanics. This has a "T-head" which gives ample leverage. In addition, a full kit should include a long-bladed and a short-bladed insulated electrical screwdriver; a pair of long-nosed pliers incorporating wire cutters and strippers; and a set of feeler gauges. For lubrication a pressure oil-can is useful and a grease gun is vital. As an investment for your motor-cycling future this should be of the high-pressure type (such as a Wanner) or if you prefer a lighter gun with cartridge loading (a Nubrex, for instance) one equipped with a high-pressure hose would be satisfactory. But a cheaper gun will do, since the Honda has only low pressure nipples.

A collection of clean tin boxes or a set of specially-made steel or plastic trays are useful for storing parts removed from the machine. Ideally, you should also have an inspection lamp—preferably of the clip-on type, since this will enable you to see what you are doing while leaving both hands free. On this score, too, a Mole wrench—which can be used almost as a portable vice—is a worthwhile addition to your kit.

Where you plan to do more than the usual amount of work on your machine you can, of course, expand your tool kit further. A selection of files of various cuts are near-essentials. So are soft-metal drifts; hardened punches; hard- and soft-faced hammers; a drill—preferably electric—with bits; and a workbench with a vice. But the great thing about a workshop is that it can be built up over the years. There's no need to obtain everything at once yet, once bought, good tools last and are rarely wasted.

USING YOUR TOOLS

Even the simplest hand tools demand rather more than merely to be placed in position and tugged hard. Each type of spanner, for example, has its own purpose and its own characteristics.

Unquestionably the great all-rounders of the tool kit are the open-enders, which are slimly built and which can therefore be slipped into confined spaces which no other spanner could reach. Their jaws are angled. That means that the spanner can be used to loosen a nut when only a few degrees of movement are possible. When the limit has been reached, the tool is removed, reversed, and room for another few degrees of movement is thus obtained.

Naturally, only the right size of spanner should be used. The open-ender is designed to exert pressure along the flats of a nut or bolt and is consequently made with jaws of just the right width for the job. Use too large a spanner and it will sit at angle, applying the full force you exert not along the flats but on two of the angles. Normally, this stress is just too much for the metal of the bolt. The spanner turns, taking with it the two corners against which it was pressing, and you are left with a rounded head which no spanner will grip. Just occasionally, the bolt bites back and springs the jaws of the spanner instead. Then you have a ruined spanner . . .

You can also damage the jaws by applying too much force when trying to free a stubborn bolt. Here, one is often tempted to slip a piece of piping over the spanner to increase the leverage, or link two spanners together by interlocking their jaws. The best advice is—don't. Such methods may succeed occasionally, but normally they will ruin either the bolt, or the spanner, or both. There is, for instance, always a danger that the bolt may be snapped in two.

Instead, try a different type of spanner—a ring or a socket. These do not operate on the flats, but on the angles, and they therefore have the advantage of exerting pressure all round the head with no danger of slipping. The same pressure applied through a ring or a socket may do the trick. If not, try the effect of jarring the thread by placing a drift against the face of the bolt head and giving a sharp tap with a hammer. Repeat this half a dozen times. If it fails, give the bolt best for the time being and swamp it with penetrating oil. Repeat the dose at hourly intervals and you will eventually find that its grip has loosened. Where nuts or bolts are obviously rusted they should be soaked with penetrating oil for some hours before an attempt to loosen them is made.

Just as there is a knack in undoing nuts and bolts, so there is in tightening them. Excessive force should not be employed, and if a torque wrench can be used to tension them to an exact setting so much the better. Otherwise, exert only full hand pressure—not arm pressure—and do so through the length of the spanner alone, not through an artificially lengthened tool. Every spanner is made to a length appropriate to the size of the nut and bolt which it is to deal with, and use of too much force may lead to fractures.

This consideration applies particularly to Hondas, where light alloy plays a notable part in the construction. Here, the steel bolt is considerably harder than the alloy into which it is threaded, and over-enthusiasm with the spanners will rip the threads in the alloy. After that, you will need to retap the hole and use a larger bolt.

Pliers, of course, should never be used as makeshift spanners—they damage the hexagons—and adjustable spanners should be reserved for emergency use, since they can never be as accurately set as the correct spanner.

Screwdriver blades, too, should be appropriate to the size of the slot in the screw heads. Don't try to force a thick blade into a fine slot; nor use a thin blade in a wide one. Either way, you'll simply damage the head. With stubborn cross-headed screws, you will find that the 'driver tends to ride out of the cross. If this happens, place a drift on the screw and give it several sharp blows with a hammer. But be very careful if you are doing this on a light-alloy component, or you may fracture it. For really stubborn screws, try the effect of local heat on the alloy—a rag soaked in boiling water may do the trick. Again, penetrating oil might help.

After use, clean your tools before they are put away. Many mechanics like to wipe them with a lightly-oiled rag after the dirt has been cleaned off. This certainly helps to preserve the tools, but remember that any oil should be dried off before they are used again. Wrap them in clean dry rag—not in plastic sheeting, for this causes rusting—hang them up in racks in your workshop, or keep them in a special tool box. Whichever course you choose, make sure that they are stored in a dry place. They will then give you service as good as that of the Honda itself.

3 Looking After your Honda

ALL the routine jobs which need to be done on the Honda twins are basically simple and can, in fact, be carried out using the standard tool kit. Of the routine work, tappet, plug gap and contact-breaker points adjustment, taking up slack in the control cables, topping up the battery and adjusting the drive chain should be carried out as soon as the daily or weekly inspection shows the work to be necessary. Lubrication—including cleaning the oil filter—and attention to the air and fuel filters should be done on an elapsed-time or mileage basis.

TAPPET ADJUSTMENT

All Models. When adjusting the valve clearances—a job which must be done with the utmost precision if full performance is to be obtained—it is essential that the engine should be stone cold. It is thus better to make

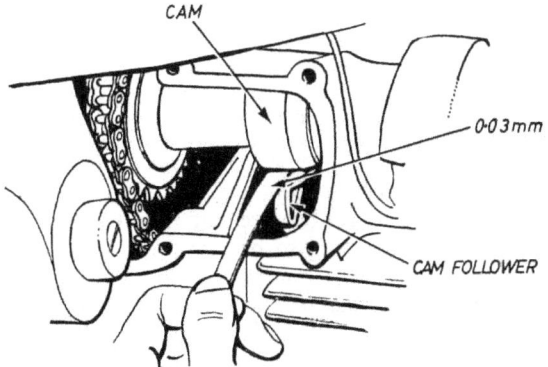

Fig. 6. Tappet adjustment on the 450 is verified by measuring the clearance between each cam and its follower, using a 0·033 mm feeler gauge. It pays to purchase a set of metric feelers if you own a Honda, since these give more exact settings than inch conversions

this the first job one morning, when the engine has stood overnight and before it has been started. If this is not possible, at least delay adjustment until the engine has had five hours in which to cool again.

Before starting the work, wipe away all dirt from the areas around the screwed rocker box caps. If the engine is very dirty, wash the grime away with paraffin or grease solvent applied with a brush. Otherwise, a vigorous wipe with clean rag will suffice. The object is to prevent dirt entering the rocker box and so being circulated through the system with the lubricant.

The actual method of tappet adjustment does not vary significantly on any of the machines. Before work can begin, the timing cover has to be detached to give access to the timing marks on the generator and casing.

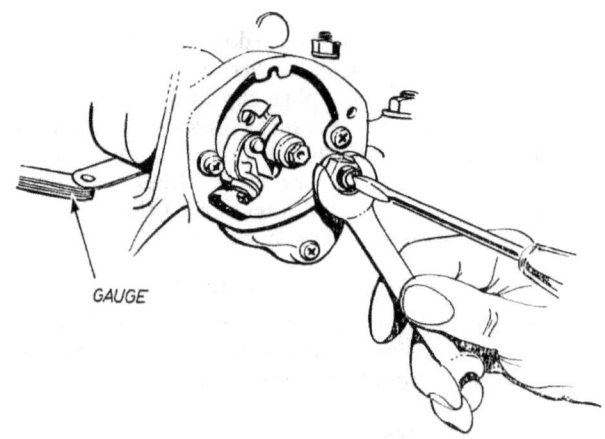

Fig. 7. Alterations to the CB.450 tappets are made by loosening this locknut and turning the adjuster with a screwdriver. Do the left-hand cylinder first, with the "LT" mark on the generator rotor aligned with the crankcase index mark. To adjust the right-hand cylinder turn the crankshaft through 180° and set the appropriate adjusters on the other side

The screwed plugs on the rocker box are then removed to bare the rockers. Some riders—myself included—also prefer to detach the sparking plugs so that the engine can be turned over more easily during the checking.

With all this done, turn the crankshaft so that the appropriate mark on the generator rotor (see the specialized chapters for details) is brought into line with the timing mark stamped on the crankcase. Then use a feeler gauge to check the adjustment of the valves. If both have no play at all it is possible that you have selected T.D.C. on the exhaust stroke instead of, as is required, on the compression stroke. To check this, turn the crankshaft one complete rotation, so that the "T" mark again comes to rest against the timing mark on the case. At least one of the valves should now have play, but if not there is a further method of ensuring that you have the right stroke. That is to watch the action of the valves as the shaft turns. If you have T.D.C. on the exhaust stroke, the rear (inlet) valve will next be fully depressed by its rocker and will then close again as you pass B.D.C. at the beginning of the compression stroke. It is then only necessary to bring the two timing marks into line to be certain that the cams are properly positioned for tappet adjustment to begin.

The recommended tappet setting for all models is given in the "Facts and Figures" section. Some are very fine—only 0·002 in.—and some dealers with long experience of Hondas normally add a precautionary thousandth of an inch to these to make the settings 0·003 in. My own preference is for the standard method. However, though there is a certain

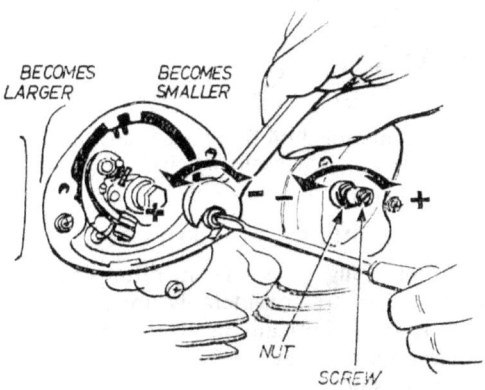

Fig. 8. When adjusting the tappets on the 450, turn the screwdriver as indicated here to make the clearances larger or smaller

amount of tolerance so far as a little extra play is concerned, there is none whatsoever for reduced clearances. The gap must under no circumstances be smaller than specified or the valves and the performance will suffer.

To adjust the valves start with the left-hand cylinder. Place the 9 mm ring spanner (supplied with the tool kit) over the lock-nut and fit the 3 mm "square" key over the end of the tappet adjuster, with a tommy bar through its hole. Release the lock-nut by turning the spanner anti-clockwise, keeping the adjuster itself steady with the key. When the lock-nut has been loosened a little, insert the appropriate feeler between the valve and the adjuster. You should be able to slide it to and fro freely. Do so, moving it about an eighth of an inch back and forth, while with the other hand you slowly tighten the adjuster. You will suddenly feel the adjuster pinch the feeler. Immediately, reverse the action and, keeping up pressure on the feeler, free the adjuster very slowly. As soon as you feel it release the gauge, stop turning, hold the key steady, and tighten the lock-nut. You should now have an exact setting, but as it is possible that the adjuster moved while being tightened you should recheck the gap. Obviously, it will not be smaller. If it were, the feeler would be clamped hard between the adjuster and the valve. Therefore, it can only be correct or too big. Try inserting the next-largest feeler. If it will not fit, then your gap is correct.

Repeat the sequence on the exhaust valve, using the feeler appropriate to the gap you have chosen. Then turn the flywheel half a turn on 180° crank models or one turn on 360° types and adjust the other cylinder. Refit the caps, the plugs and leads, the timing cover, and the job is done.

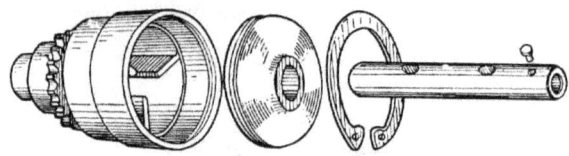

Fig. 9. This type of centrifugal oil filter is employed on the earlier Honda twins. To clean it, the securing circlip must be released

PLUGS AND POINTS

Checking the Sparking Plug Gaps. Temperatures inside the combustion chambers of your Honda are considerably hotter than those in the oven in your kitchen. It may seem all the more incredible, then, that it is possible to maintain a set gap between two thin metal points under such conditions. In fact, it is not only possible but vital, for though a plug will work with a gap which is almost wildly incorrect the engine will not give of its best under such conditions. Regular checks on the plug gaps are, therefore, one of the essentials of maintenance.

Such a check is easy to carry out. Working on each plug in turn, detach the plug cap—it simply pulls off—and unscrew the plug from the head, using the box spanner which is supplied in the tool kit. On new machines you may find that the plugs are a very tight fit indeed, and under these circumstances it is permissible to tap the tommy bar gently but sharply with a hammer to help free the plug. Be careful, though. Don't let the hammer slip and hit the cylinder or head, or it may fracture the fins. And don't let the spanner cant over, or the blow may fracture the porcelain insulator of the plug.

Make sure, as you take the plug out, that you do not lose the copper washer. This washer has two important jobs to do. First, it provides a gas-tight seal at the plug/head joint. Secondly, it allows the nose of the plug to project into the combustion chamber by just the right amount. Without the washer the nose would be too far in, and the build-up of carbon around the threads thus exposed could make the plug very difficult to remove at some later date.

Once the plug is out, use feeler gauges inserted into the gap to measure the clearance between the electrodes. The exact gap is specified in "Facts and Figures," and if there is any significant variation the gap will have to be reset. But there is another factor to be taken into account, and that is the *condition* of the plug itself. It is useless setting the correct gap between two electrodes if one is burned away to a point and the other is severely pitted. So, unless the plug is obviously in good condition, I prefer to clean it first and square off the centre electrode with a fine file. When that has been done I can see if it is worth bothering with that particular plug at all, or whether it would be better to fit a new one.

Cleaning the Plugs. It is possible to clean the plugs yourself, using a stiff-bristled brush or a wire brush. In the latter case, however, try to

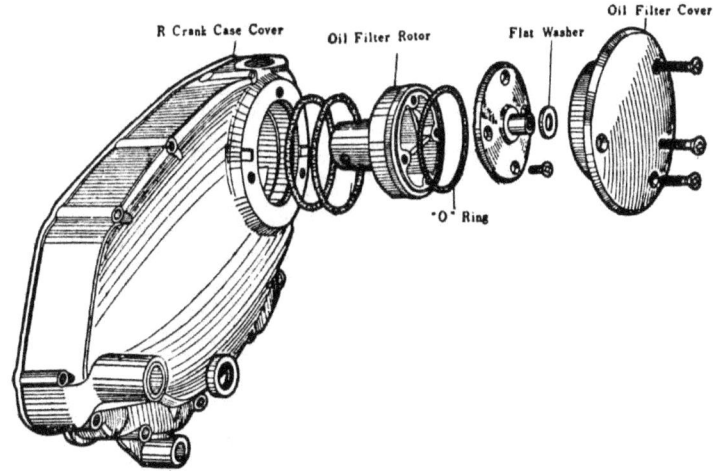

Fig. 10. Four countersunk screws hold the end of the oil filter element on the 125 c.c. twins. Cleaning is similar to that of the bigger machines

confine your attentions to the metallic parts—the plug body, the side electrode and the centre electrode. If the wire brush comes into contact with the insulator nose there is a danger of metallic traces being deposited on the nose, possibly leading to a high-tension leakage. The better method is sand-blasting on a garage rig. However, if you do have this done make certain that the garage gives the plugs a thorough cleaning with compressed air afterwards so that all sand particles are blown out, otherwise these might fall into the bores.

The ideal is that the insulator nose, the plug body, and the faces of the two electrodes should be absolutely clean. The metal parts should be shiny. Don't forget that it is the underside of the side electrode which counts—the upper surface can be as brilliant as chromium plating, but if the side facing the centre electrode is dirty and pitted the plug will not be fully efficient. When you are satisfied with its condition, you can pass on to the actual gapping. If you are not satisfied it is far, far better to fit a brand-new plug instead. They are cheap enough, and the extra efficiency is worth the slight cost involved.

Setting the Plug Gaps. First of all, check the existing setting on each plug and note if it is too wide or too small. If it is wide, leave the correct feeler gauge in place and very gently tap the top of the side electrode, using the flat of a light spanner. Slide the gauge a little. It should move freely sideways, but not up and down. Try inserting the next-highest

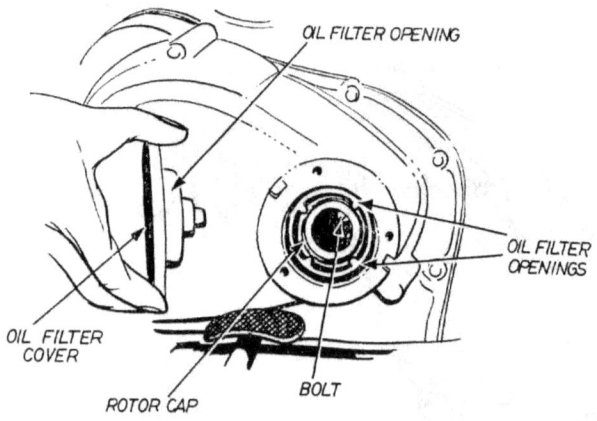

Fig. 11. How access is gained to the filter on the 450. Similar arrangements are employed on other models

gauge. It should be too big to fit. If it is not, tap the electrode again and re-test. Within a few tries, you should have the exact setting.

A gap which is too small must be opened up. This can be done by bending the electrode with a plug gapping tool, or by shifting it gently with the blade of an electrical screwdriver. In the former case, the gauge is inserted from the side; in the latter, the screwdriver blade is eased in from the open end. Take great care not to touch the centre electrode as you do this, for it is essential that it should not be bent. Keep checking the gap as already described, until it is exactly right. The plug can then be refitted to the head.

Fitting the Sparking Plugs. This is one of those deceptively easy jobs which aren't as simple as they may appear on the surface. Before a plug is inserted, for example, it pays to smear a little oil or very light grease over its threads. This will make it easier to get it out again next time.

The sealing washer, too, must be in good order. The idea behind these washers is that they should not be fully flattened—just a little "spring" should remain to provide a gas-tight seal. If the existing washer has been

LOOKING AFTER YOUR HONDA

crushed flat it will not make an efficient seal. Use a new one—you *can* purchase them separately without actually buying a new plug!

When offering a plug up to the head, be careful not to strike the electrode against any part of the engine. The reason is obvious—the blow could be enough to bend the electrode slightly and therefore alter that gap you have just set so carefully. And don't overtighten the plugs. Giving a final wrench "just to make sure it's tight" may result in a warped plug body and a gas leak. The correct procedure is to insert the plug by

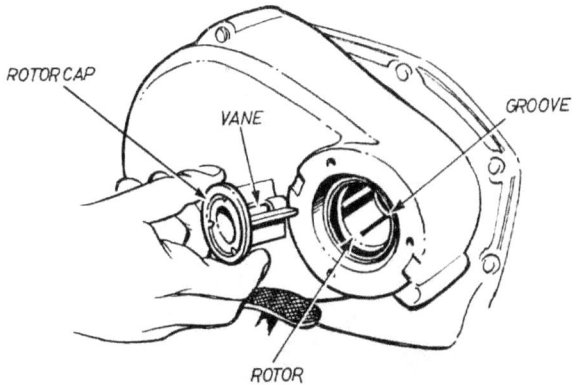

Fig. 12. The filter element removed from the 450. It is of a slightly different design to that on the earlier models

turning the box spanner with your hand alone—no tommy bar—until it feels fully tightened. Then fit the tommy bar, and give the spanner half a turn to crush and tension the washer. And that should be sufficient.

Refit the plug caps after wiping away any dirt which may have accumulated inside them. And wipe the whole length of the plug leads, too. Make sure that when each cap is fitted, no part of it is in contact with the cylinder head, since it has been known for H.T. current leakage to take place through a cap, and being in contact with a mass of metal might accentuate this.

THE STARTER MOTOR

Starter motors are something of an unknown quantity to motor-cyclists. In fact, owing to the comparatively short periods of use they require very little attention. To keep them in good order, however, it is advisable to check the brushes and commutator, and to grease the gear casing, every 6,000 miles.

The brushes are set under a removable cover on the starter motor body. Detach this (with the motor on the bench) and loosen the two bolts holding the brush carrier plate. The brushes are held by springs. Check that they are not unduly worn, and that the segments of the commutator are not flush with the mica. If they are the mica must be cut back. This *can* be done with a section of broken hacksaw blade, but it is a job best left to an electrical workshop.

Over-running Clutch. The screech of the Honda's electric-starter over-running clutch soon becomes familiar to owners. It is normal, and need not therefore be a cause for alarm. This clutch is a sturdy mechanism and it is inadvisable to disturb it.

LUBRICATION

Periodic Lubrication. All Models. Besides regular oil changes, there are lubrication schedules to be carried out on all machines. These involve such moving parts as the fork-link pivots and front damper pivots. The links are given a shot of grease through each nipple—there are four of

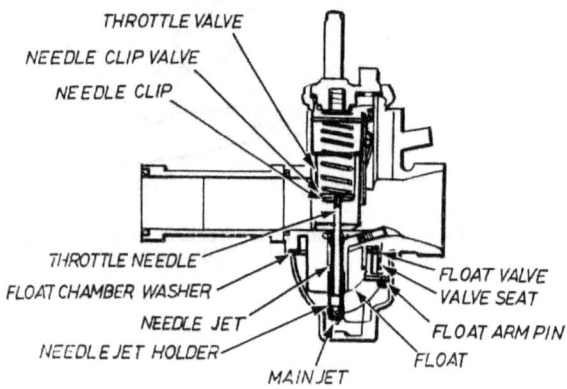

Fig. 13. The basically simple needle-jet carburettor is employed on all models except the 450, and the later 125 which is not sold in Britain. This is a typical example, as fitted to the 160 c.c. machine

them, plus a fifth on the brake plate for the speedo drive—once every 3,000 miles.

The cables are lubricated by being freed from their controls at the handlebar end, and having oil injected down the inner wire, using a pressure can. Be generous with the oil, since smooth-acting controls are vital and, in any case, you will also prolong the life of the cables. But a word of warning—under no circumstances must you oil the speedometer cable. If you do, it will act as a pump and inject the oil into the speedo-meter, which will then be damaged.

Besides these points, there are a number of others which will repay a spot of oil now and again. The best method is to start at the front and work backwards. So, first of all attend to the greasing of the suspension and oiling of the cables. Then give any exposed carburettor linkages a little oil. Lubricate the pivot of the footbrake, the anchorages of the return spring, the stop-lamp spring and the stand-return spring. The brake clevis should also be lightly oiled, as should the kickstarter pedal's pivot bolt and spring on the folding mechanism. Oil the clutch-operating lever pivot, too.

Don't oil rubber-bushed pivots—such as those on the rear dampers. Here, either use nothing at all or else apply a silicone spray. But don't overlook the drive chain. On some models this works under good conditions in its case, but it will probably appreciate an annual lubrication.

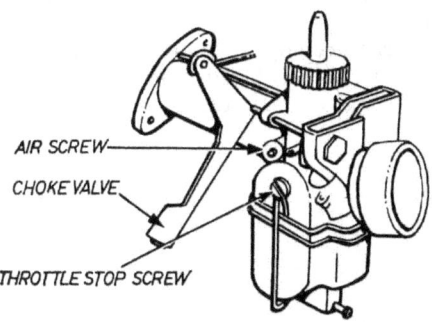

Fig. 14. Adjustments to the carburettor are normally confined to setting the air screw and the throttle stop—but before you start work ensure that the choke valve is fully open

You can lightly oil the lower run through the inspection hole in the case, rotating the gear wheel so that the whole chain is covered.

On the sports models, with their open chains, this lubrication must be more thorough, and the chain will have to be cleaned before lubricant is applied. Remove the chain by detaching the left-hand crankcase rear cover (normally held by three screws) and turn the wheel to bring the spring link into a handy position. Ease the horseshoe-shaped spring off by gently lifting one end out of its groove with a screwdriver and pressing the spring away from the link. The side plate can then be withdrawn, and the rest of the link pushed out to break the chain. Place it in a tray and wash it thoroughly in petrol until it is absolutely clean. Then hang it up to drain dry, placing a folded newspaper underneath it to catch the drips, which will otherwise stain your garage floor.

When it is completely dry, test it for wear by extending it, on its side, and picking it up. Even a new chain, under this test, will take up an arc, but a worn chain will fall into a quarter-circle. If it has worn to that extent, it means that the chain and the sprockets should be renewed.

If you are to use it again, examine all the links for cracked or broken rollers and plates. If you find any, break the chain at the affected point by use of a chain tool—it is simply a clamp equipped with a screw plunger which presses out the rivet—and fit a new link.

I recommend using Linklyfe to lubricate the chain. This is a special graphited grease which comes in a large flat tin. Merely put a loop of wire through one link of the chain, roll the chain up, and place it on top of the lubricant. Set the entire tin on a gas ring or electric stove and allow the grease to melt. The chain will sink into it. Allow it to immerse itself completely, then remove the tin from the heat. Use plenty of thick rag to hold it—it will be hot! Lift out the chain, hang it over the tin to drain, and when it is dry you have a perfectly lubricated chain whose rollers are packed with grease. It is a clean and painless way of doing a normally rather messy job.

At intervals, you can keep up the good work by treating the chain while it is actually on the machine with brush-on Linklyfe—a special type which contains a solvent to make it suitable for brush application.

4 Be your own Doctor

If, feeling off colour, you visit your doctor you do not expect him to treat you by haphazardly amputating your leg, your arm, or your tonsils. Were he to attempt to do so, you would soon be on the look-out for a new medical man. Yet not a few riders treat their machines in just that way—and apart from refusing to work altogether there is nothing that the long-suffering motor-cycle can do about it.

When an engine goes sick, or an electrical system breaks down, the way to cure it is to adopt the same approach that you would expect from your own doctor—a methodical examination with all the symptoms weighed up, followed by a logical diagnosis which accords with the facts.

Take the engine first. Here you can make one basic assumption. If the correct charge of mixture is induced at the proper time; is compressed; is fired by a spark occurring at the correct instant; and if the residue is properly exhausted then the engine *must* work. If it is not working it proves that one of these basic requirements is not being met, and you must carry out an examination to discover why.

The first stage must be the obvious one—a check on the fuel supply. Is there fuel in the tank? If so, is it reaching the carburettor? You can test that easily enough by depressing the float chamber tickler and seeing if petrol floods from the carburettor after, say, 10 seconds. If it doesn't the fault is some form of fuel stoppage—you may even have forgotten to switch the tap on, or have failed to set it to "reserve" on a low supply. Or, a filter may be blocked. Detach the pipe from the carburettor and see if petrol flows steadily through it. If it does, you know that the stoppage must be in the carburettor itself—and presumably in the needle valve. If it doesn't, or if the flow is intermittent, it can mean that the pipe is blocked; that the tap or filter is blocked; or that the fuel tank air vent in the cap is blocked.

Check the pipe itself by detaching it from the tap and then moving the tap to the "on" position. If fuel emerges in a steady flow you obviously have a blocked fuel pipe on your hands—a proposition you can confirm by simply attempting to blow through the pipe with your mouth. If it is blocked. you can clear the stoppage by the judicious use of a piece of wire.

Where the pipe passes muster, check the cap vent by removing the cap altogether. The result should be a steady flow through the tap. Again, no flow means that the only other possibility—the blocked tap—is the answer. Clearing it will probably involve detaching the complete tap, and before doing so it is best to drain off all the fuel. You can prevent fuel loss, however, by completely sealing the filler orifice with cellulose tape. If no air can enter no fuel can leave, and the tap can then be detached and opened up for cleaning.

Where the initial check showed that fuel was reaching the end of the pipe but not entering the carburettor, the next step would be to turn off the petrol and remove the carburettor for examination. The fault could only be a needle valve blocked with dirt—which could be cleaned by flushing it in petrol—or a valve which was jamming because of a mechanical fault. It might, for example, have been bent through careless reassembly—by a previous owner, of course! Here, replacement by a new part would be the only viable course of action to take.

There are three other types of fuel problem. One is over-flooding—evidenced by dripping from the carburettor when the tap is switched on, and by misfiring and lumpy running if the engine works at all. Again, only the float/needle valve assembly can be responsible for this. The valve may be prevented from closing by dirt; the float may be leaking, in which case it will not lift the needle enough to shut off the supply; or a damaged needle may not be seating properly. Check all three points.

Then there is failure of the fuel to pass through the jets. Again, the cause is likely to be dirt which has become trapped in the very fine passage which constitutes a jet. Such trouble often takes the form of an engine which will start, but which will not continue to run when the throttle is opened or which will run but which will not pull under load. Stripping out the jets and examining them is the procedure. If you find one which is blocked, holding it to your lips and blowing through it in the reverse direction to that in which the petrol flows will normally dislodge the dirt. If this fails, you may be able to poke it clear with a bristle—or, in an emergency, use a piece of thin wire. True, this may easily damage the jet: but, since it is not worth being stuck on a lonely road half the night for the sake of a sixpenny jet, I would certainly use whatever means were to hand to clear it and then replace the jet at the earliest opportunity thereafter.

Where an initial check on the fuel system discloses no obvious faults, the next stage in fault tracing should be to test the ignition system and, more especially, to examine the sparking plugs themselves. To a knowledgeable rider the plugs can often tell a revealing tale of conditions in the engine. If the nose of a plug is covered with soft black soot it usually means that the engine has been running over-rich. If, on the other hand, the nose and insulator have an ash-white appearance it denotes hot running, which in turn infers that the mixture is too weak. Here, one can again think in terms of fuel starvation and blocked jets. Hard glazed carbon on a plug shows that oil is being burned—possibly due to a worn bore, faulty rings or leakage down the inlet valve guides. But normal combustion is indicated by coffee-coloured plugs.

Your first sight of the plugs, therefore, will have given you several clues about the conditions inside the engine. Closer examination will tell you more. If, for example, a plug has not been firing at all it is likely to be wet with fuel. But don't take that on trust. Even if it is dry, you should reconnect it to its H.T. lead, place it in contact with the metal of the cylinder, and switch on the ignition. Then, keeping the plug body well in contact with the engine, kick the unit over. A fat blue spark should jump across the gap between the plug's electrodes each time the kickstarter is operated. No spark indicates an ignition fault, and your next step is to find out exactly where it is. First of all, eliminate the plug itself from your list of suspects by fitting a brand-new plug in its place and carrying out the spark test all over again. If the new plug sparks the inference is pretty

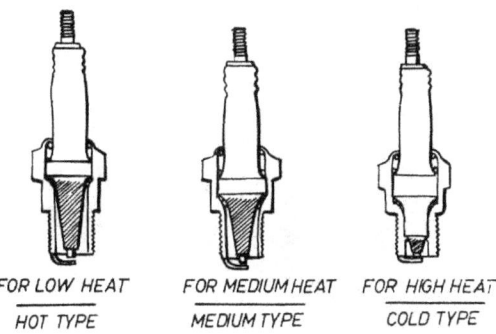

Fig. 15. The three basic types of plugs, designed to give maximum efficiency under various operating conditions. A hot plug is used in a cool-running engine; a cold plug in one that runs hot. For general use a medium plug is recommended. The major difference is in the length of the insulator nose

obvious. But if there is still no spark the fault must be in the generator the contact-breaker, the plug lead, or the cap.

Even though the old plug sparked, the trouble may still be solved by fitting a new plug. The reason is that a plug which works when tested out of the engine may still be faulty when fitted and subjected to the pressures existing in the combustion chamber. Once the plug's efficiency has been established beyond all doubt, carry on by testing the plug lead.

To do this, you will need a long piece of wire—a nail even. Insert this so that it makes electrical contact in the plug cap, and position it so that it is about an eighth of an inch from the bare metal of the cylinder head or barrel. Keeping it there, operate the starter. You should obtain a spark across the gap. If you fail to do so, unscrew the cap from the lead and jam the wire or nail into the hole in the centre of the lead into which the cap was screwed. Then repeat the test. Either you will get a spark or you won't. If you don't, then the fault lies deeper in the system. If you do, it proves that the cap was faulty. You can often cure this by cleaning the inside of the cap—this tends to accumulate dirt, which eventually leads to tracking—or, where it is already clean, by chopping a quarter of an inch or so off the H.T. lead so that the cap's screw bites into fresh core. Re-test after each operation.

Where the plugs and caps have been checked without result, turn your attention to the wiring. Test all leads and terminals for security and proper insulation. You should always carry with you your handbook containing the wiring diagram. Use this to help in your check on the wiring. The ignition switch itself may be faulty. Here, one indication is whether or not the neutral-indicator light comes on when the ignition

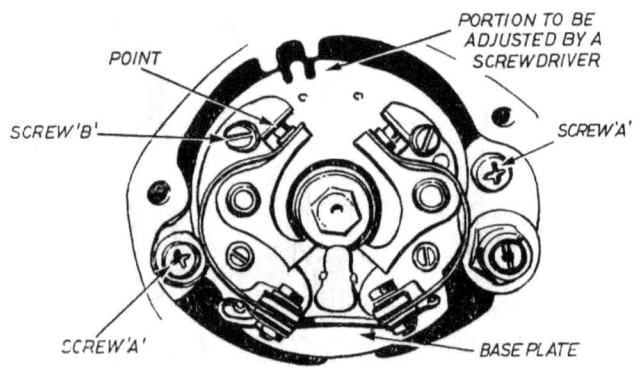

Fig. 16. A typical contact-breaker unit—the type used on the 450. The ignition timing is checked by setting the "LF" mark on the rotor against the crankcase index mark, at which stage the points should just begin to open—a gap of 0·0015 in. With the points fully open the gap should be 0·3–0·4 mm (0·012–0·016 in.). Adjust by loosening the screws 'A' and moving the base plate by means of a screwdriver inserted in the adjuster slots. Tighten the screws afterwards, and recheck the gaps. For accuracy, it is better to use a stroboscope to check the timing—really a job for a garage

switch is operated with the gears in neutral. If it does, it suggests that the switch is in order.

A complete electrical check by the wayside is, of course, out of the question. Only one immediate possibility remains—to test the contact-breaker and timing. With the points fully open, measure the gap between them. If it varies significantly from the recommended setting readjust and see what effect this has. Clean the points, too, by inserting a piece of clean card or paper and closing the points so that they just—but only just—grip it. Then carefully pull it out; select a fresh area; and repeat the operation until the paper is clean on withdrawal.

Lastly, check that the points are breaking at the correct point. The timing marks will give you the datum which you need, and if there is any significant variation you can easily re-time the spark.

The only other "simple" fault which could cause such a complete electrical failure is flooding of the electrics with water—as might occur if the machine has been charged into a flooded patch. Here, the cure is to dry the system out by soaking up the moisture with clean rag. Otherwise, the conclusion must be that the fault is a fundamental one—failure of the coil, perhaps—which can only be tested and rectified by a garage.

Mechanical defects severe enough to lead to engine failure are rare indeed, and are likely to be the results of some other fault rather than first causes. On the other hand, they *will* stop the machine . . .

Failure to keep the oil level correct and to change the lubricant at the proper intervals can, for instance, lead to seizure. This, in turn, may break the rings. When that happens the compression will be insufficient to enable the mixture to be burned properly, and the engine will not run. Loss of compression can easily be felt through the kickstarter—there is little or no resistance as the engine is turned. Where broken rings are suspected it is essential that the engine should be turned over as little as possible, since the sharp ends of the snapped rings can play havoc with the surface of a bore, and can completely ruin it within minutes. Any sudden loss of power coupled with heavy blue smoke from the exhaust is likely to be due to ring breakage, and action should be taken accordingly.

A gradual loss of compression is more likely to be caused by a tappet which is tightening itself, and so holding one or other of the valves off its seat. If it is an inlet valve which is not seating properly the unit will tend to spit back through the carburettor. If an exhaust valve is affected there will probably be back-firing and rumbling in the exhaust. In either case, idling is almost certain to be unreliable and the unit will probably tend to overheat.

Running with a tight tappet can cause damage—and not just to the valve and its seat. Local overheating may distort the cylinder head/barrel/crankcase joints and in severe cases may even result in a hole being melted through the crown of a piston. An emergency adjustment should therefore be made. It is impossible to set Honda tappets accurately with the engine hot, but you can at least ensure that the valve is freed by finding T.D.C. with both valves at rest and then setting the adjusters so that the tappets have just a slightly perceptible play with the valve fully seated. This is, of course, a "get you home" measure, and as soon as the unit is cold the proper settings should be made.

Blockage of either the induction or exhaust systems is highly unlikely, and providing both valves are seen to be operating and the compression is sound it can safely be assumed that mixture is being induced, compressed and the residue exhausted. That being so, any mechanical failure would be of the order of slipped valve timing or an actual breakage of a valve, spring, tensioner or chain. None of those faults can be corrected at the roadside and garage assistance will therefore be needed.

Transmission faults are more straightforward—either the drive is being transmitted or it isn't, at least as a general rule. But mild clutch slip may

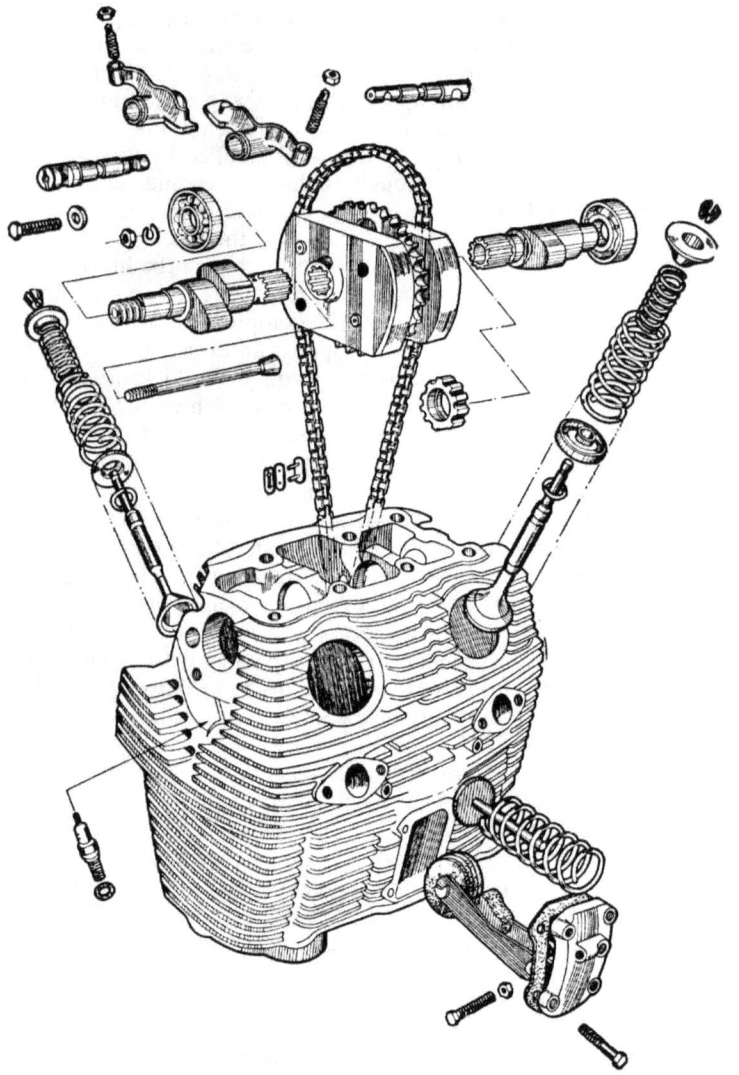

Fig. 17. How the valve gear is arranged on the 250 and 305 c.c. Honda twin motor-cycles

sometimes give the impression that the engine is losing power. The easiest way to check this is to snap the throttle open on a steep gradient, listening very carefully to the exhaust note. If it rises sharply, but without the machine itself gaining speed, it is a sure sign of clutch slip. This can be caused by maladjustment, or by worn plates or tired springs. If the adjustment proves to be correct then the clutch will have to be stripped for new parts to be fitted.

A process of elimination can also be applied to the lighting system. Here, the lamp *must* light if electricity is present and there is a full circuit. If it doesn't light, it proves that there is either no electricity or else a faulty circuit. I have found, from experience, that Japanese bulbs are not up to the engineering standard of Japanese engines. Bulbs which on visual examination seemed to be in good order were in fact duds, the wires inside the body having failed and caused an open circuit. Before going any further, therefore, I would always suggest substituting a new bulb for the original one to see if that is the part at fault. If it isn't, take the checking a stage further.

For this, you will need to have your wiring diagram so that the circuits can be traced. The fault for which you are looking may be one of two kinds—a short circuit or an open circuit. Electricity will always take the shortest path to earth: it will not flow unless there is a complete circuit.

Think of it rather like a railway. If there has been a bad bit of points setting, the train which should have reached your station has instead been diverted on to a different line. That's a short circuit. If, on the other hand, a bridge has collapsed your train has not arrived because it is standing on the other side of the gap and can't come any further. That's an open circuit. Of course, there's the third possibility that the train has been cancelled and isn't running. That is equivalent to there being no electricity at all.

The simplest way to check is to see whether any of the lights operate at all. If *all* bulbs are "dead," with the engine running, you have a major electrical failure on your hands. What is more likely, though, is that you will find that some light and others don't, arguing a faulty circuit. Having decided, therefore, what you are looking for you can proceed with your check. It will be much easier if you are carrying with you a simple test rig—a length of wire connected to a bulb holder at one end, with a darning needle soldered to the inner core at the other; and a long length of cable equipped with crocodile clips at each end.

Using your wiring diagram as a guide, trace the circuit backwards from the faulty component towards the source of power. If you find the wiring diagram depressingly like a small-scale plan of Hampton Court maze, try tracing out the one circuit you want with a pencil, remembering that what the diagram doesn't show is the earth return which makes up the second half of the circuit.

Work back along the lead, examining it for signs of broken insulation which could result in a "short." An open circuit, caused by a break in the wire core which may not have fractured the insulation, is more difficult to trace. Here, the bulb holder rig is useful. Earth the holder, switch on the current, and press the needle through the insulation at intervals along the wire. Don't thrust it right through. It need penetrate only enough to touch the inner wire. If the wire is "dead" your test bulb will not light. When the wire is "live" it will. When you come off a "dead" area on to a "live" one you have localized the area of breakage, and you need only probe a little more to find the exact spot. The insulation can then be cut, the inner wire joined, and the joint wrapped with insulating tape.

At a pinch, you can by-pass a whole section of wiring by connecting your jumper lead—that's the one with the crocodile clips—direct from the power source to the component which you want to use. You will still have to trace and rectify the fault later on, but at least it can be done in the comfort of your own garage. Here, too, any temporary wire repairs which you have carried out can be made permanent. Rather than leaving a fractured wire twisted and taped together, it should have a snap connector soldered or crimped into place, together with a proper insulating sleeve.

You may, of course, find that loose terminals are responsible for either loss of contact altogether or for an intermittent contact. If this is so, clean them thoroughly and in the case of snap connectors tighten them by judiciously-applied pressure with a pair of pliers.

When making electrical repairs at home, remember that as a general rule a soldered joint is always to be preferred. The only exception here is if a bared wire is to be locked into a terminal by means of a grub screw, binding the ends with solder may result in the screw working loose and making the joint insecure. Here, the screw should be well locked down so that it crushes the wire strands hard against the terminal, and so ensures good electrical contact.

So much for the generalities of trouble tracing. Having learned the methods involved, you can combine item with the detailed diagnoses set out in the following Chapter to equip yourself to pinpoint any fault which may afflict your machine.

5 Trouble Tracing the Easy Way

IN practice, not much goes amiss with a Honda. Even so, when the thing *does* stop it helps to have a ready-reference guide to what the fault may be, to back up one's own powers of deduction explained in the previous Chapter.

Here is Honda's own official trouble-shooting sequence for the CD.175. It is, of course, equally applicable to other models in the range.

ENGINE TROUBLE

Situation	Probable Causes	Action
Engine starts but will not keep running	1. Fuel tap blocked 2. Filler cap vent blocked 3. Tappets wrongly set 4. Air leak in carburettor manifold joint 5. Incorrect oil level	Inspect parts. Clean and adjust as required
Engine misfires when warm	1. Faulty plug 2. Defective coil 3. Float chamber fuel level incorrect	1. & 2. Substitute new parts 3. Adjust level
Engine smokes at high speeds	Oil is reaching the chambers past worn or damaged pistons, rings, or bores	Strip engine for inspection and renew any faulty parts. Rebore may be needed
Noises from upper part of power unit	1. Piston slap due to wear 2. Worn big-end 3. Tappets incorrectly set	1. Strip for measurement 2. Strip for check and fit new big-ends 3. Check setting
Engine overheats	1. Needs decoke 2. Dirty plugs 3. Wrong plugs or gaps 4. Drive chain dry or too tight 5. Oil level low; wrong grade of oil 6. Points gap wrong; points dirty or burned	1. Decarbonize 2. Check, clean plugs 3. Check and adjust 4. Lubricate chain and adjust 5. Check level. Change oil if necessary 6. Examine points. Replace clean or adjust as necessary
Engine will not start and lacks compression	1. Object caught between valve and seat 2. Tappet too tight	1. Remove tappet covers to check valve operation If necessary, remove head to check 2. Check and adjust all tappets

TROUBLE TRACING THE EASY WAY

ENGINE TROUBLE (Contd.)

Situation	Probable Causes	Action
Engine will not start, compression O.K.	1. Ignition timing wrong 2. Blown fuse	1. Check and adjust 2. Fit new fuse
Engine runs, but stalls	1. Fuel tap blocked 2. Blocked fuel passage in carburettor 3. Fouled or wetted plugs 4. Ignition timing wrong 5. Blown fuse	1. Remove pipe to check fuel flow 2. Remove and flush carburettor 3. Fit spare plugs 4. Check adjustment 5. Fit new fuse. If old fuse is faulty, the pilot lamp will not light up
Oil emulsifies, more especially in winter	1. Water in oil 2. Wrong oil used 3. Clogged breather	1. Drain and flush 2. Refill with recommended oils 3. Clean breather pipe
Fuel consumption rises (related symptoms:—low exhaust note; reduced pressure at exhaust outlet; low compression when kick-starting)	1. Clogged air cleaner 2. Contact-breaker points dirty or wrongly gapped 3. Carbon in head or exhaust system 4. Timing retarded 5. Wear on pistons, rings and bores	1. Renew element 2. Reface and clean points. Regap 3. Decarbonize thoroughly 4. Check timing. It is retarded if points open after timing mark "F" on rotor is passed 5. Overhaul engine
Loss of r.p.m.	1. Clogged fuel passage 2. Fouled plug 3. Clogged air cleaner 4. Ignition timing wrong 5. Silencer fouled	1. Check plugs. If dry and ashen, flush out carburettor to give proper fuel flow 2. Clean and gap plugs 3. Remove element and fit new one. Black smoke from exhaust suggests a clogged element 4. Check and adjust 5. Remove silencer and clean out carbon
Poor throttle response	1. Cable not properly adjusted 2. Air cleaner clogged 3. Exhaust pipe or port blocked by carbon 4. Ignition timing wrong 5. Tappet adjustment wrong	1. Check cable setting 2. Fit new element 3. Remove pipe and decarbonize 4. Check timing 5. Check tappet setting
Distributor points burned	1. Oil on points 2. Timing wrong 3. Faulty condensor	1. Clean points and cure oil entry 2. Check timing and adjust 3. Have condensor tested electrically

CARBURETTOR TROUBLE

Situation	Probable Causes	Action
Fuel overflows. Related symptoms: poor idling, poor speed performance, excessive fuel consumption, bad starting, poor pulling power, poor acceleration	1. Dirt in fuel	1. Remove float chamber cover, remove float, check for dirt around needle valve. Clean with compressed air, or by stripping valve. Clean in petrol and reassemble
	2. Worn or damaged needle valve-seat	2. Replace valve and seat with new parts
	3. Punctured float	3. Remove float and shake. Listen for petrol. Or immerse in water at 90–95°C (194–203°F) for one minute. Bubbles indicate a puncture
	4. Float arm lip bent	4. Straighten lip and reset float to give correct fuel level
Poor idling. Related symptoms: poor low speed performance, bad pick-up, poor performance at moderate speeds	1. Air screw badly set	1. Close screw, and count turns. For correct setting see Facts and Figures section. Start engine and turn screw up to a quarter turn each way from this position to point where engine revs highest but smooth
	2. Throttle stop setting wrong	2. Back off screw all the way; check throttle operation; reset screw
	3. Blocked jets for slow running	3. Unscrew cover plug and remove pilot jet. Blow away dirt. Remove and clean slow running jet
Poor performance at intermediate speeds. Related symptoms:—flat spot, poor acceleration, excessive fuel consumption, poor pick-up	1. Clogged slow running jet or pilot jet	1. Deal with as above
	2. Throttle needle set incorrectly	2. Remove slide and set needle in third notch
	3. Fuel level wrong	3. Check, clean and if necessary renew needle valve; reset float if necessary
	4. Clogged air vent tube	4. Clean out vent
Poor high-speed performance. Related symptoms:—loss of power, poor acceleration, black exhaust smoke, lack of response	1. Main jet loose or blocked	1. Remove main jet; clean; fit securely
	2. Air vent tube blocked	2. Clean vent tube
	3. Choke not fully open	3. Check that choke opens fully
	4. Fuel tap not fully open	4. Check that tap opens fully
	5. Throttle needle loose	5. Inspect needle locking clip. If broken, fit new one
Poor starting	1. Too much choke	1. Dry out plugs and start up with choke fully open
	2. Too much fuel	2. Check main jet, as above
	3. Fuel tap not fully open	3. Check action of fuel tap

TROUBLE TRACING THE EASY WAY

ENGINE NOISES

Situation	Probable Causes	Action
Tappets noisy	1. Excessive clearances 2. Tappets worn	1. Readjust to the standard setting 2. Regrind, or renew
Piston slap	1. Worn bores or pistons 2. Excessive carbon 3. Wear in small-ends	1. Rebore unit 2. Full decoke 3. Renew faulty parts
Noisy cam chain	1. Tensioner adjustment incorrect 2. Chain stretched 3. Sprocket teeth worn	1. Reset adjuster 2. Renew chain 3. Fit new sprockets
Knock from clutch	1. Wear on plate abutments 2. Clutch centre spline worn	1. Fit new plates 2. Renew centre
Knock from crankshaft	1. End play excessive 2. Faulty bearings	1. Overhaul assembly 2. Fit new bearings
Kickstarter chafes	1. Oil seal friction	1. Dismantle for inspection
Noisy contact-breaker	1. Defective heel on arm	1. Renew

STEERING FAULTS

Situation	Probable Causes	Action
Bars hard to turn	1. Race overtightened 2. Damaged bearing balls 3. Head stem bent	1. Reset adjustment 2. Renew balls and tracks 3. Fit new stem
Handling poor	1. Loose bearings 2. Bent rim 3. Spokes loose 4. Rear fork pivot bush worn 5. Frame twisted 6. Chain adjusters mis-aligned 7. Defective tyre	1. Check for wear and renew as necessary 2. Re-tension spokes 3. Re-tension or renew 4. Fit new bush 5. Have frame jigged 6. Readjust to set rear wheel straight 7. Examine covers for bead or side wall damage. Check tyre pressures
Machine pulls to one side	1. Front or rear suspension out of balance laterally 2. Fork leg out of line 3. Forks misaligned 4. Rear fork deformed 5. Front axle bent 6. Loose components	1. Renew fork leg or spring unit 2. Renew faulty leg 3. Reset alignment 4. Renew fork 5. Renew axle 6. Check security of all steering and suspension units

CLUTCH FAULTS

Situation	Probable Causes	Action
Slipping clutch	1. Springs weakened 2. Plain plates worn or warped 3. Friction plates worn or warped	1. Fit new springs 2. Fit new plain plates 3. Fit new friction plates

CLUTCH FAULTS (Contd.)

Situation	Probable Causes	Action
Clutch does not disengage	1. Excessive wear on friction plates 2. Incorrect adjustment	1. Reline or replace 2. Reset to standard recommendation
Clutch drags	1. Distorted plates 2. Clutch springs unevenly tensioned	1. Strip, examine and renew as necessary 2. Check springs and reset or renew

GEARCHANGE MECHANISM

Situation	Probable Causes	Action
Gears fail to engage	1. Selector drum lug broken 2. Selector arm lug broken 3. Uneven motion between drum and selector fork 4. Damaged selector fork 5. Dogs on layshaft gears damaged 6. Dogs on mainshaft gears damaged	1. Strip and renew 2. Strip and renew 3. Remove to grind down high spots 4. Strip and renew 5. Strip and renew 6. Strip and renew
Pedal does not return to central	1. Return spring broken 2. Spindle fouling case or cover	1. Renew spring 2. Strip for examination and repair
Gears jump out of engagement	1. Worn dogs on layshaft gears 2. Worn dogs on mainshaft gears 3. Selector fork worn or bent 4. Selector drum stopper spring damaged	1. Strip and renew 2. Strip and renew 3. Strip and renew 4. Strip and renew

FRONT AND REAR SUSPENSION

Situation	Probable Causes	Action
Springing too soft	1. Weakened springs 2. Excessive load carried	1. Replace springs 2. Reduce weight of luggage
Springing too hard	1. Front dampers faulty 2. Rear dampers faulty	1. Inspect dampers 2. Inspect dampers
Noises from suspension	1. Damper casing rubbing 2. Casings foul springs 3. Bump rubber damaged 4. Damper oil level too low	1. Inspect and align 2. Align 3. Renew 4. Top up

BRAKING SYSTEM

Situation	Probable Causes	Action
No adjustment left	1. Brake shoes worn 2. Operating cams worn 3. Cam "slippers" worn	1. Fit relined shoes 2. Renew cams 3. Renew
Noise on brake application	1. Linings worn 2. Grit embedded in lining 3. Brake drum surface pitted 4. Cam spindle bush worn	1. Inspect and reline 2. Fit relined shoes 3. Remove for skimming 4. Rebush backplate

BRAKING SYSTEM (Contd.)

Situation	Probable Causes	Action
Brakes inefficient	1. Seized cable	1. Remove and lubricate. Eradicate any sharp bends
	2. Loose brake rod	2. Inspect all pivots
	3. Shoe contact only partial	3. Inspect for high spots and ease by filing
	4. Dirt or water in brake	4. Dismantle for cleaning
	5. Oil or grease on brake linings	5. Fit relined shoes. Do *not* attempt to renovate old brake linings

DRIVE CHAIN

Situation	Probable Causes	Action
Chain stretches rapidly	1. Excessive load applied	1. Avoid "snatch" gear changes
Excessive wear	1. Worn or damaged sprockets	1. Renew chain and *both* sprockets
	2. Wrong sprocket in use	2. Check, and renew

6 Doing a Decoke

THERE are two main objectives behind doing your own maintenance work—unless, of course, you are already a keen amateur mechanic. One is to save time. The other is to save money. Where there is no significant economy in either, I believe in letting the professionals take over.

In the case of the Honda twins much of the saving is open to question, since in some instances a set of special tools are required. Whether or not it is worth buying these to tackle a job which you are likely to do only once during your ownership of the machine (if then, for Hondas are notably reliable) is very doubtful. On the other hand, you may cause damage if you attempt the work without them.

My advice, in cases such as this, is to carry out what I term a "peripheral overhaul"—to confine your own work to those parts which are readily accessible with the normal run of tools. Since this takes care of perhaps ninety per cent of the jobs likely to arise it is, to my mind, the most logical and economical method.

DECARBONIZING

A "decoke" is the commonest job of the lot—one which has quite wrongly acquired a reputation of being something of a panacea. "If the engine isn't running well, decoke it" perhaps sums up the general view.

It's the wrong view, too! You gain nothing by disturbing the engine unnecessarily. First of all, check *why* the engine isn't running well. Then, if it seems to be a likely cure, by all means carry out a decoke. But it is not a cure-all, and may even aggravate certain complaints, at least temporarily.

The object of a decoke nowadays, when fouling and carbonizing has been so notably reduced by oil and fuel additives, is to attend to the valves— the "lungs" of a four-stroke engine. These are of the utmost importance— they *must* be in good condition if the unit is to work well. If their seats are burned and pitted, their stems encrusted with carbon, or their springs weak, they cannot provide an effective gas seal and the engine cannot work at full efficiency.

For a decoke, you need the tools to remove the head and valves; a scraper; a small wire brush; a valve grinding tool; some fine grinding paste; a pint of petrol; a stiff brush; some grease solvent; and a few containers in which to place parts as you remove them.

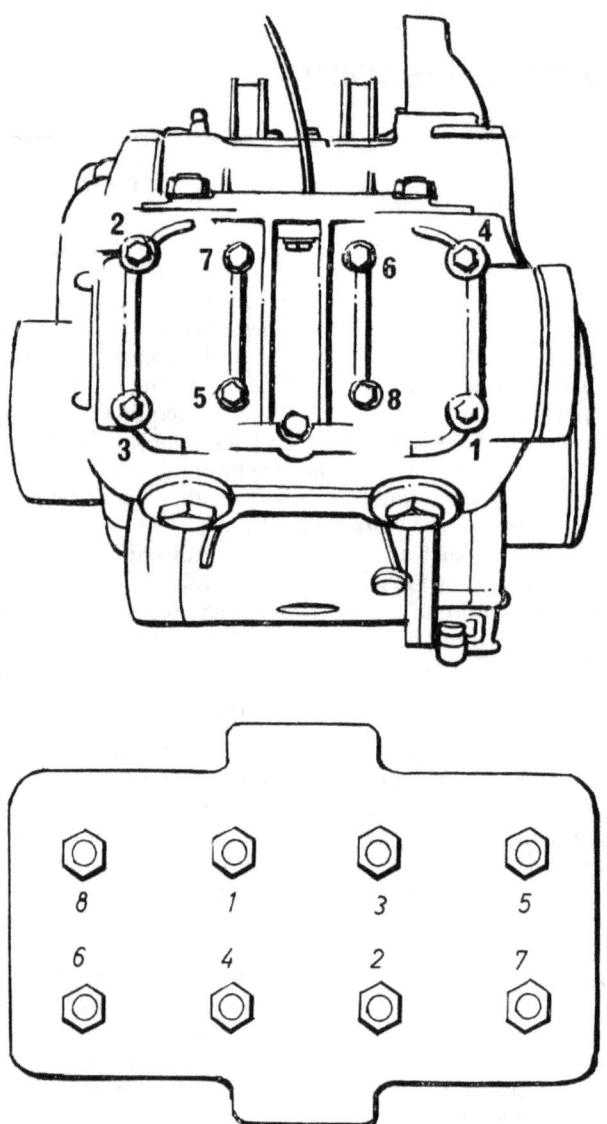

Figs. 18 & 19. When re-tightening head nuts a sequence should be used. As examples, here are (*above*) that for the 160 c.c. machine and (*below*) for the 450

DOING A DECOKE

Begin by cleaning the outside of the engine thoroughly. Brush grease solvent all over it, working it well into the fins and paying particular attention to the underside. Then gently hose it away, and dab the engine dry with rags. You can now start work.

Detach the carburettor and the exhaust pipe. Then remove the head. (The detailed instructions for doing this on the various models are given in the specialized chapters). Hold the barrel steady with one hand while you bring the pistons to T.D.C.—one piston at a time on 180° engines. And don't lose the cam chain down the tunnel!

Using your scraper, remove any carbon from the piston crowns. Many riders like a ring of carbon to be left round the top circumference of pistons, since this acts as an oil seal on older engines. The best way of ensuring this is to press an old piston ring against the top of the piston so that it just wedges in the barrel. Then use the scraper to cut the carbon up to the edge of the ring. Give a final clean-up with the small wire brush. You can, if you wish, polish the piston crowns with metal polish too. This has no effect on performance, but it does make it harder for carbon to adhere to the surface, since a polished area offers less of a "key." But you must ensure that no metal polish strays from the crowns into the bores.

Now you can work on the head. Before removing the valves, scrape and wire-brush all the carbon out of each combustion chamber. Leaving the valves in place protects their seats from accidental scratching. Don't forget to pick any carbon out of the plug hole threads too. You can do that with a stout needle. When the head and valves are clean, you can finish these off with metal polish, too.

Next, remove the valves so that their seats can have attention. For this, you will need a valve spring compressor, though it is possible to "make do" by shaping a block of hardwood to fit inside the head and butt against the valves. With this placed on the bench, one can press on the valve collars and so free the collets. Detach the collars and the valve springs and remove the valves for inspection.

Before working on the valves themselves, finish off the head—now that the ports are unobstructed—by cleaning out the exhaust sections. Work from the pipe end, scraping and polishing until all carbon has been removed. Apart from the occasional attention to the exhaust pipes and silencers that is all the actual "decarbonizing" which needs to be done.

The valve seats and faces will need to be washed in petrol before grinding-in commences. It may even be necessary to take them both to a Honda agent for cutting. Pits up to 0·006/0·007 in. deep can be ground out. Any deeper than this will call for refacing. As it is difficult to measure the depth of a pit-mark accurately, the best bet is to reface if there is extensive pitting, or to grind in if there is not. If refacing is necessary, both the seats and the valves will have to be cut to an angle of 45°.

To grind in the valves, smear grinding paste round the seating face of the valve and drop it back on to its seat—without the spring fitted, of course. Insert a broad-bladed screwdriver into the slot in the valve head and, pressing gently down, oscillate the screwdriver between your hands to turn the valve back and forth on its seating. After about a dozen strokes lift it up and turn it through 90°—a quarter of a turn—and then drop it back and repeat the process. Carry on with this grinding until both valve and seat show an unbroken grey line of contact. Before you can see this, you will have to wash them in petrol. If the line is not complete, dry them and smear on fresh grinding paste. Then continue until you get

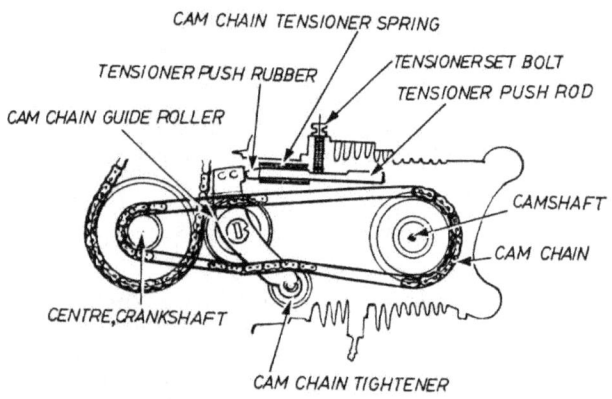

Fig. 20. Cam chain tension is important. Here is the layout—shown horizontally for ease of presentation—on the 160 c.c. model

the desired result. Repeat the process with the second valve. Then attend to the other combustion chamber in the same way.

You can now replace the valves. Always use new valve springs after a top overhaul—springs weaken with use; and replacements are cheap. When the valves and springs have been refitted, test the efficiency of your valve seating by pouring into each port in turn enough petrol to cover the valve area to a depth of about half an inch. Then use a tyre pump to pressurize the petrol slightly. If none is driven through to the combustion chamber side the seating is perfect. If petrol is able to pass through, however, so can gas—and the valve spring should be removed, and the faulty seating ground yet again until a leak-free seal is obtained.

Rebuild the engine, and it should be good for at least another 10,000 miles before the work need be repeated.

7 Working on the C.92 and C.B.92

AMONG the earliest Hondas to be imported, the 125 c.c. Benley models—the C.92 and the CB.92—gave many British riders their first introduction to Japanese motor-cycles. Many are still on the roads, although the early two-bearing crank tended to be somewhat fragile. The later three-bearing machines are more likely to be encountered.

Engine Removal

1 Remove the footrests. On the C.92 these are formed from a single cross-bar which is bolted at four points to the underside of the crankcase. Footrests on CB.92 models are individual units mounted on plates bolted to either side of the machine. Before the CB.92's left footrest can be detached the gear-change linkage must be released.
2 Detach the exhaust systems. Take off the complete pipe/silencer assembly on each side as one unit.
3 Detach the carburettor covers and the tool box cover.
4 Unbolt the tool tray base and pull out the air cleaner element which is fitted to the inside of the circular cover. Release the element from the carburettor hose by slipping the left hand inside the frame, through the carburettor aperture, and unhooking the hose clip.
5 Release the nut which secures the wiring junction box and then free the clamp. Undo the various snap connectors.
6 Take off the rear section of the left engine cover to gain access to the chain. Disconnect the chain link to break the chain. Then detach the inner section of the cover as well.
7 Release the clutch cable from the control arm.
8 Detach the carburettor.
9 Take off the battery cover, unscrew the clamp bolt and the two terminal bolts, and remove the battery.
10 Release the starter solenoid switch from the frame and disconnect the starter motor cable.
11 Take off the kickstarter.
12 Remove the sparking plug caps from the H.T. leads and ease the leads out of their channels in the cylinder head.

13 Make up a suitable engine support from wood blocks or a stout box and insert it under the crankcase.
14 Take off the nuts from all engine mounting bolts. These are in order: No. 1 bolt in front of and above the rear fork pivot, No. 2 bolt in the upper mounting atop the head, and No. 3 bolt in front of and below the rear fork pivot. Nos. 1 and 3 occur on both sides of the frame.
15 Detach both No. 1 bolts and then both No. 3 bolts.
16 Detach No. 2 bolt. The engine is now free to be lifted on to the bench.

Head Removal

1 Remove the contact-breaker cover and disconnect the green wire from the terminal on the plate.
2 Detach the left crankcase cover. If the recess-headed screws are difficult to undo, jar the threads by a sharp blow from a hammer applied to a soft-metal drift placed on the screw heads. Be careful when jarring threads on screws which have no supporting metal around them.
3 Remove the left-hand-threaded 8 mm bolt holding the auto-advance mechanism. Use a hammer to tap the spanner *anti-clockwise*.
4 Remove the alternator rotor. An extractor is required for this. It is possible, however, to utilize the rear-wheel spindle for this job. After the rotor has been removed take out the Woodruff key from the shaft.
5 Remove the four 6 mm bolts holding the starter motor to the front of the crankcase and the two clamps holding the starter cable under the crankcase. That done, twist the motor's sprocket end towards the alternator to free it from its chain. Alternatively merely remove the starter sprocket circlip and leave the motor place.
6 Detach the ignition coil from the right side of the crankcase (applicable only to engines up to No. C.92 E-937064).
7 Remove the five cross-headed screws which secure the alternato base plate. This can then be withdrawn, complete with starter chain and sprocket. If the alternative method of removing only the circlip was adopted in step 5 the motor sprocket will come away with the chain.
8 Remove the cam chain tensioner pivot bolt and detach the arm. This is made easier if the cam chain tensioner adjustment screw on the crankcase is first screwed fully home.
9 Rotate the crankshaft until the cam chain link comes to the point where the tensioner's rubber roller previously rested. Remove the link to break the chain.

WORKING ON THE C.92 AND C.B.92   41

10 Remove the six cylinder head cover nuts and slide the head from its studs.

Removal of Valve Gear

1. Detach the left side cover on the head and turn the cam sprocket until the chain is free.
2. Unscrew the three securing bolts and detach the sprocket.
3. Loosen all tappet adjusting screws.
4. On early engines the head carries a distributor. Remove this. On later engines take off the right cylinder head cover.
5. Remove the circlips which locate the rocker shafts.
6. Drive out the rocker shafts using a soft-metal drift.
7. Pull out the camshaft from the drive side opening.
8. Using a valve spring compressor remove the valves. Number them for identification.
9. Decarbonize in the normal way.

Replacing Head and Re-timing

1. Reverse the stripping procedure to reassemble the head components. Use a new gasket and a little jointing compound to make an oil-tight joint at the right cylinder head cover plate. When re-installing the camshaft sprocket, note that the bolt hole nearest the timing mark on the sprocket is offset. Therefore, the holes must be accurately aligned before inserting the bolts.
2. Replace the chain, and rotate the sprocket until the inlet side of the chain is six inches longer than the exhaust side.
3. Refit the head. For the purposes of identification the head nuts are considered to be numbered. They are identified as follows (looking at the engine from the rear, as it would be seen by a normally-seated rider): front, left to right, Nos. 5, 1, 3. Rear, left to right, Nos. 4, 2, 6. Of these, No. 6 is a domed nut which must be sealed with a little jointing compound. Tighten all nuts to finger tightness first. Then lock them up a few threads at a time in the same order as their numbers. If a torque wrench is available it is best to use it. The correct torque for the nuts is 10 ft. lb. minimum and 15 ft. lb. maximum.
4. To time the engine set the "O" mark on the camshaft sprocket alongside the notch cut on the cylinder head. Then turn the crankshaft sprocket so that its timing mark is right at the bottom, but on an extension of a line passing through the two cam sprockets. Join the cam chain at a point adjacent to the crankshaft sprocket, making sure that the spring link is replaced with the open end facing the crankshaft sprocket.
5. Replace the cam chain tensioner, turn the crankshaft slightly in the direction of normal rotation, and loosen the adjuster bolt until

the tensioner guide separates from the bolt's lower end. Then tighten the adjuster lock-nut, and complete the reassembly of the lower half.

Clutch Removal

1. Remove the eleven screws which secure the right crankcase cover.
2. Detach the oil filter cage from the end of the crankshaft.
3. Undo the four 6 mm bolts which retain the clutch centre plate, and remove the springs and friction plates.
4. Pull out the thrust button from the clutch centre.
5. With a pair of circlip pliers, remove the circlip which is set into the end of the main shaft. Pull out the clutch centre.
6. Take out the oil pump mounting stud and its securing bolt.
7. Pull out the clutch body complete with oil pump; remove the thrust washers, and separate the pump plunger arm and piston from the oil pump body.
8. To free the arm from the clutch remove the securing circlip.
9. Take off the left crankcase cover, remove the 6 mm bolt holding the clutch adjuster and detach it from the cover. Unhook the clutch lever spring from the cover.
10. Unscrew the clutch-operating quickthread from the adjuster.

Clutch Reassembly

1. Fit the 20 mm thrust washer on to the transmission shaft, position the oil pump gasket and install the assembled clutch body and oil pump as a unit. Then fit the clutch centre and secure with its circlip.
2. Insert the clutch plates, starting with the single B-type plate. Follow this with, alternately, a friction plate and a plain A-type plate. There are four friction plates and three "A" plates.
3. Insert the pushrod and thrust button. Add the clutch springs and the pressure plate and tighten down with the four 6 mm bolts.
4. Refit the oil filter and replace the right crankcase cover.
5. Reassemble the adjuster and quickthread into the left-hand case. Refit the quickthread return spring. Replace the casing.
6. Give several shots of grease through the nipple feeding the operating mechanism.
7. Test and readjust the clutch.

Stripping the Gearbox

1. Invert the engine, after removing all components from the left- and right-hand crankcase sides—and undo the nuts and bolts holding the upper and lower crankcase halves. Lift away the lower half, and unhook the kickstarter return spring. The main and layshafts and the kickstarter spindle can then be lifted out of

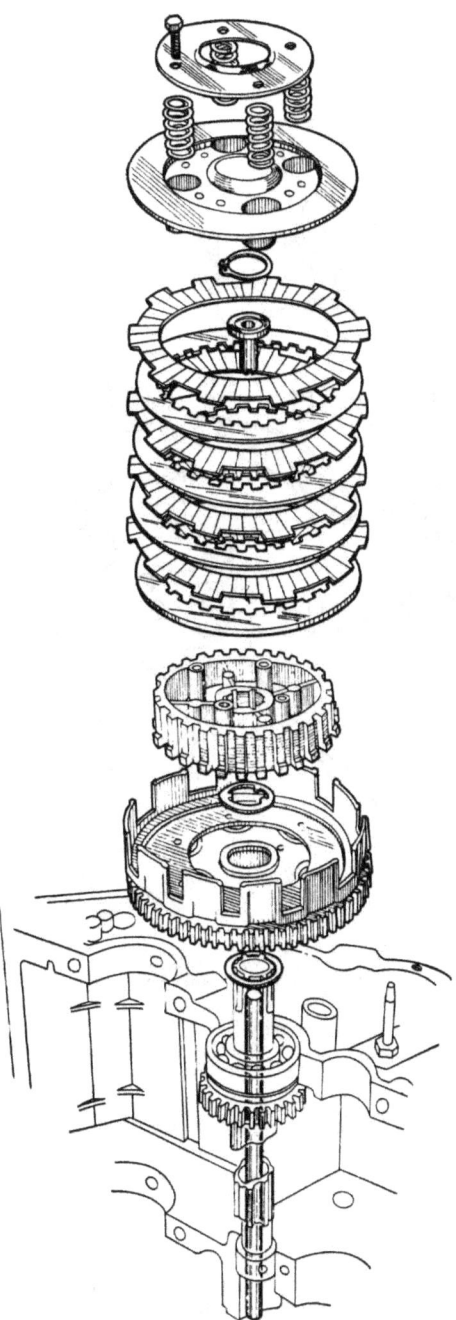

Fig. 21. This is the type of clutch used on the 125 c.c. C.92 motor-cycle

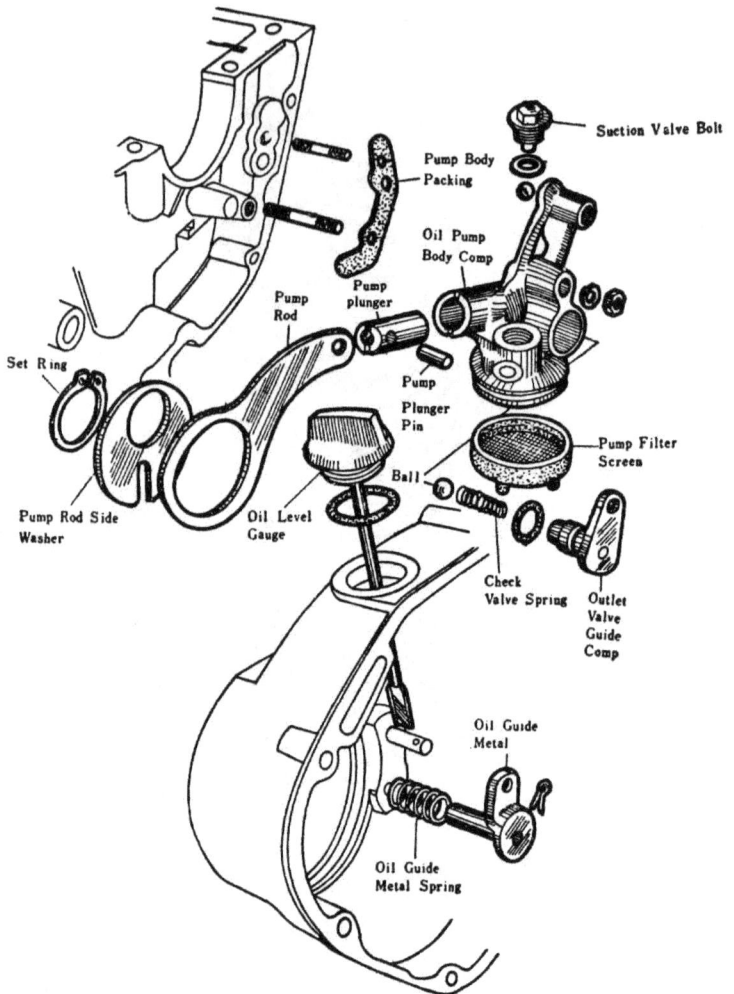

Fig. 22. Operation of the oil pump by an eccentric on the clutch body is an unconventional feature of the twin-cylinder machines. This is the 125 c.c. layout

the upper section of the case. Circlips are used on both main and counter shafts to hold, respectively, the second and third gears. The final drive sprocket is bolted into place.

2 A circlip on the left of the selector drum spindle forms the location for this component. Remove this, press the forward-facing

selector link on the right-hand side outwards, and tap the left-hand end of the spindle until this link does not interfere with the gear lever arm guide. Then detach the bolt on which the (rear) stopper arm is pivoted and lift out the arm.

3 Next, the selector drum guide roller must be taken off. On early engines (before C.92 E-12001) this was incorporated in a single bolt on the upper case. Later engines and CB.92 and CA.95 machines have a more complicated device held by two bolts.

4 Flatten the selector fork tab washers, detach the guide pins, detach the neutral indicator switch from the end of the selector drum, and extract the drum from the case.

Reassembly involves a simple reversal of this procedure, using normal fitting methods.

8 Working on the 160 c.c. unit

As with the earlier twins, the engine must be removed from the frame before any serious work can be done.

Engine Removal

1. Having made sure that the fuel is turned off, remove both exhaust systems. This involves detaching the finned clamps at the cylinder head, removing the four 8 mm bolts which hold the footrest assembly, and the 8 mm bolts which secure the silencers to the pillion footrest mountings.
2. Now take off the air cleaner cover and the tool box.
3. Disconnect all electrical leads joining the engine to the frame. The low-tension wires are released at a snap connector cluster behind the unit, just under the left-hand air filter. The starter motor cable is freed from the switch just under the dual seat on the left-hand side, and the high-tension leads to the plugs are disconnected by pulling off the plug caps and then freeing the cables from their guides.
4. Unbolt the air cleaner tube from each filter.
5. Remove the set screws holding the rear left-hand crankcase cover, and free the clutch cable from the operating lever on the crankcase.
6. Rotate the rear wheel until the spring link on the rear chain is almost on the final drive sprocket. Then detach the link and allow the two ends of the chain to hang free.
7. Taking care not to bend the choke rod, undo the nuts which hold the carburettors to the cylinder head. By detaching the fuel pipes and the mixing chamber tops—tape these to the frame out of harm's way—you can then take off the carburettors complete with their manifolds.
8. Place a stout wooden box or blocks of wood under the engine, leaving a sufficient gap to enable it to be dropped.
9. Detach the engine mounting bolts—two 8 mm bolts on the upper mounting on the cylinder head; the lower of the two 10 mm through-bolts on the rear engine plate; and then the upper rear through-bolt. The unit can then be lowered on to the support and lifted to the bench.

WORKING ON THE 160 C.C. UNIT 47

To refit the engine to the frame, simply reverse this procedure—again using blocks of a box as an intermediate support for offering the unit up. Note that replacement of the upper mounting bolts is made easier when a T-handled socket spanner can be employed. You can, however, use a long thin box spanner with a tommy-bar instead.

Head Removal

1 First, thoroughly clean the engine. You can best do this by using a de-greaser such as Gunk, which is brushed on, or an aerosol spray can of Holts' Engine Clean. Paraffin is effective, but messy. Whichever method you adapt, however, make certain that the exterior of the unit is thoroughly cleaned before you attempt to dismantle it. That way, you obviate any risk of dirt entering the unit and damaging the delicate internal working surfaces.
2 Start the dismantling by detaching the cylinder head cover. This is held by four domed nuts—one at each corner—and by four ordinary nuts in the centre. All are 8 mm.
3 Detach the three recess-headed screws which hold the generator cover.
4 Turn the rotor to bring the cam chain spring link to the top of the camshaft sprocket. This is more easily done if you first remove the sparking plugs.
5 Detach the spring link, and attach thin twine or wire to each end of the cam chain to make reassembly easier.
6 With the cam chain out of the way, the head may be pulled off its studs. If it sticks, jar the head joint very gently with a block of softwood. In severe cases, run penetrating oil down each stud and allow it to soak for an hour before attempting to lift the head again.
7 Detach the distributor cover and undo the screws which hold the entire contact-breaker assembly to the head. There are two of these—both recess head screws.
8 Now insert a wooden wedge vertically between the camshaft sprocket and the front face of the camshaft tunnel. This will prevent the camshaft turning. The centrifugal advance/retard mechanism can then be unscrewed from the shaft.
9 Detach the four recess-headed screws which hold the points base housing to the cylinder head. It also "doubles" as a camshaft bearing support.
10 Detach the cover from the other side of the cylinder head, and take off all four tappet covers.
11 Withdraw the rocker shafts—four of them—and make a careful note of the correct position of their oil grooves so that you can reassemble them in the correct position.
12 With the rockers and their shafts out of the way, push the camshaft towards the distributor side until its other end comes free.

Then tilt it upwards, and draw it out of the head through the aperture left by the cylinder head cover.
13 Carry out decarbonizing as described in Chapter 6.

Replacing Head and Re-timing

1 Reassemble the unit by reversing the dismantling sequence. Use new gaskets throughout, and take care to line up the oil holes in the rockers with the oil grooves on the shafts by inserting—temporarily!—an 8 mm bolt through each inner stud hole to act as end stops for the shafts.

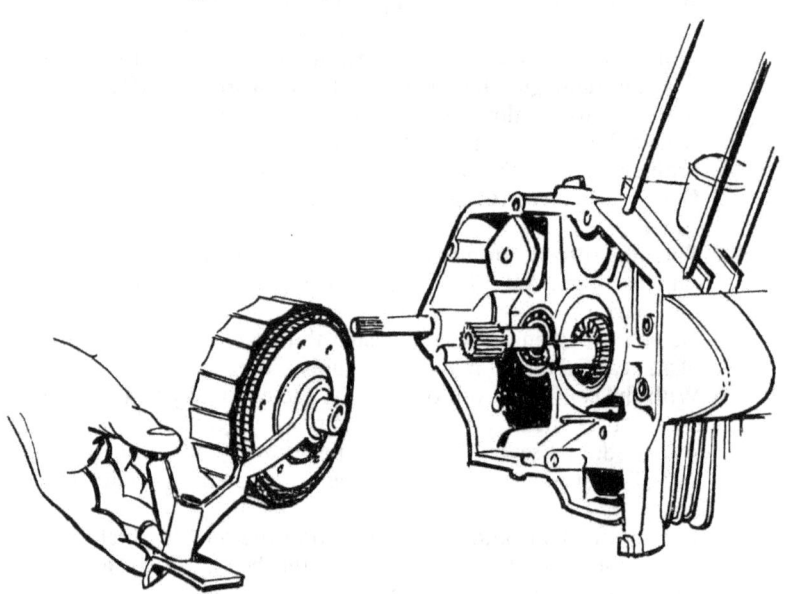

Fig. 23. How the oil pump comes away with the clutch body. This is on the 160 c.c. engine, but the others are similar

2 Refit the head, using the wire or twine on the cam chain to feed it through the tunnel. Then re-time the valves by turning the rotor until the "T" mark aligns with the pointer which you will find at "10 o'clock" on the starter. Without moving the rotor, turn the camshaft to bring to the top the tooth which carries a pop mark on its right-hand side, and engage the chain with the sprocket. Replace the link, remembering that the closed end of the spring clip must face the direction of rotation.
3 Complete the rebuilding of the engine, tightening the head nuts down in the order shown on p. 36—a little at a time—using

WORKING ON THE 160 C.C. UNIT

a torque wrench to set them to a maximum of 15 lb. ft. and a minimum of 10 lb. ft.

4 With the rotor set at the "T" mark, check the valve tappet clearances. These should be 0·004/0·006 in. (0·10–0·15 mm). Before carrying out this check, adjust the cam chain by loosening the lock-nut on the adjuster bolt, set between the cylinders at the front of the engine, and then the bolt itself. The chain then adjusts itself automatically. When this has been done, re-tighten the lock-nut.

5 Adjust the ignition timing by setting the rotor so that the "F"

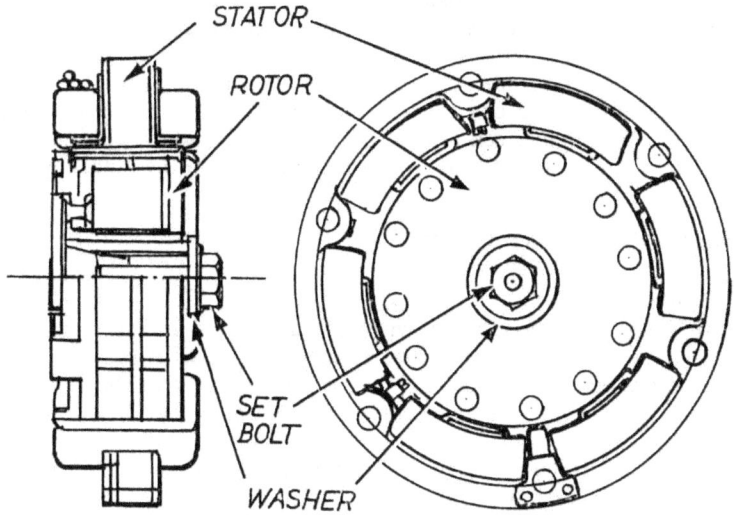

Fig. 24. Typical layout of the generator unit

mark lines up with the stator plate pointer. When this is done, the points should just be beginning to open. This is best checked by means of a timing light, which should extinguish itself the instant the points break. When fully open, the points should have a gap of 0·012–0·016 in. (0·3–0·4 mm).

6 To reset the timing, the two screws holding the base plate should be loosened just enough to allow the plate to be moved. If the points are opening too early—i.e., the ignition is too far advanced —turn the plate anti-clockwise. If they are opening too late (retarded ignition) turn it clockwise.

7 The points gap is reset after the timing has been adjusted and the base plate screws tightened down. The two screws holding the contact-point plate are loosened slightly, and a screwdriver is inserted in the eccentric slot on the plate to adjust the gap to

within the stated tolerance. The screws are then re-tightened and the gap checked once again.

Cylinder Removal

1 After removal of the cylinder head, detach the single bolt at the rear of the camshaft chain tunnel, and draw the cylinder block off its studs. As the pistons emerge from the barrels, support them so that they are not damaged.
2 Cover the crankcase mouths with clean non-fluffy rag, and then ease the circlips out of their recesses in the pistons. The gudgeon-pins holding the pistons can then be pushed out. Mark the crown of each piston so that you will know on which side to replace it.
3 If you wish to remove the cam chain tensioner, loosen the tensioner lock nut and undo the 10 mm set screw completely. The thrust bar and spring can then be removed from the camshaft tunnel. On the engine, release the two 6 mm bolts which hold the "see-saw" guide roller/cam chain tensioner unit to the crankcase, and lift it away.

Reassemble in the reverse order.

Piston Rings

1 When detaching piston rings be careful not to exert too much outward pressure on them, or they will snap. It pays to have a spare set of rings handy—just in case. Note that the two upper rings, though similar in design, are not identical. The third ring is a wide scraper type.
2 When fitting new rings, first insert them squarely in the appropriate bore, one at a time. This is best done by placing the piston inside, inverted, so that its skirt comes within half an inch of the top. Use this as a guide to position the ring. Then insert a feeler gauge into the ring gap and measure it. With all rings the maximum permitted gap is 0·11 in. (0·30 mm). Where the gap is more than this, the ring must be discarded. Where the gap is less than 0·004 in. (0·10 mm) it should be carefully dressed with a fine file to open it up.
3 The working clearance in the piston groove is also important. With the grooves freed of carbon and the rings inserted, you should be able to insert feeler gauges in between the ring and the top of the groove in each case. The permitted tolerances are 0·0016–0·0028 in. (0·04–0·07 mm) for the top ring; 0·0004–0·0016 in. (0·01–0·04 mm) on the second ring; and on the oil control ring. Replacements are definitely required when the vertical play exceeds 0·006 in. (0·15 mm).
4 Before pistons are re-inserted in their bores, the ring gaps should be staggered so that they do not line up. Compress each ring in

WORKING ON THE 160 C.C. UNIT

turn as it is fed into the mouth of the cylinder. Better still, use proper piston ring compressors.

Clutch Removal

1 The clutch is set beneath the right-hand crankcase cover, which must first be removed. To do this, detach the kickstarter and then free the ten recess-headed screws which hold the cover to the crankcase.
2 Remove the four 6 mm bolts which hold the pressure plate, and take off the plate and the clutch springs. Detach the mushroom-headed release button.
3 Detach the 20 mm circlip from the clutch centre, and draw out the centre hub, the five plain plates and the five friction plates.
4 Detach the oil filter rotor from the crankshaft. To do this, grip its cross-rib with a pair of pliers and draw it squarely away from the oil filter body. Bend back the tab washer of the 16 mm lock-nut, unscrew the nut, and pull the rotor off the crankshaft.
5 Draw the primary drive pinion off the crankshaft.
6 Unbolt the oil pump, and pull the pump and clutch drum away as one unit.
7 Drive out the pump-plunger pin to separate the pump from the clutch.
8 Detach the 26 mm circlip behind the clutch drum, and remove the pump rod.

To reassemble, simply reverse the sequence.

Checking the Oil Pump

Whether or not the oil pump is working properly can be checked without dismantling simply by loosening the domed nuts at the rear of the head on both sides of the engine. If lubricant is seen, the pump is operating satisfactorily. If not, remove the pump as described here, and check the following points—

1 The operation of the plunger in its cylinder.
2 The condition of the oil pump gasket.
3 The condition of the steel balls on both the intake and delivery sides of the pump.
4 Whether the mesh filter is blocked or damaged
5 If any oil passages are blocked.
6 Whether the oil filter itself is fouled.

Splitting the Crankcase

1 Drain the oil from the unit, remove the engine from the frame, take off the right and left crankcase covers, and detach the oil

pump and the clutch. When detaching the left crankcase cover the gear lever and neutral indicator switch leads must be removed. The stator of the A.C. generator will come away with the cover.

2 Remove the cylinder head and the cylinder. Leave the pistons attached to the connecting rods, and place wood blocks between their skirts and the crankcase mouth. Gently turn the rotor until the pistons are held firmly against the blocks. Then—using the special extractor tool—draw off the rotor complete with the starter clutch. This is held to the rotor by three screws. Do not lose the key which locates the rotor on the crankshaft.

3 Now detach the 6 mm screw holding the neutral switch stator, and take this off. Separate the rotor from the gear shift drum by undoing the 6 mm screw which secures it. When reassembling this component, take care to match the rotor slot with the key in the drum.

4 Disconnect the starter motor chain at its spring link, removing the 6 mm screw holding the starter motor set plate, and detach the sprocket from the crankshaft. Free the starter leads, and detach the starter motor.

5 Release the bolts holding the final drive sprocket, and slide it from its splines. Then detach the pistons.

6 Remove the 8 mm and 6 mm nuts from the top right-hand side of the crankcase. Then invert the unit, and remove the seven 8 mm plain nuts and single 8 mm domed nut from the underside. Then detach the remaining two 6 mm nuts and five 6 mm bolts.

7 Disengage the gear-change arm from the gearshift drum—this assembly is on the kickstarter side of the engine, just in front of the kickstarter spindle—and with the crankcase still inverted gently draw the lower section away from the upper. The crankshaft and gear shafts will remain in the upper part of the case. To remove them, simply lift them out.

It should not normally be necessary to detach the selector mechanism, but where this is desired flatten the tab washer and remove the gear shift fork guide pin and the guide pin screw which is located just behind the oil filter orifice in the upper crankcase. Take out the guide collar, and remove the 6 mm stop bolt which is set just behind the gearshift drum in the right upper crankcase. You can then slip the drum out through the right-hand side of the case.

Reassembly is a simple reversal of this procedure, but note that the selector mechanism must be reset as shown in Fig. 25 and that the crankcase joint must be remade with non-setting jointing compound after being thoroughly cleansed.

9 Working on the 175 c.c. unit

LIKE the other models in the Honda twin range, the popular CD.175 A has an inclined parallel twin power unit which forms an integral part of the frame. Therefore, the engine/gearbox unit must be removed completely before any major work can be done on the top end.

Removing the Engine
1. Having ensured that the fuel tap is turned to the "off" position, remove the petrol pipe.
2. Disconnect the H.T. terminals from the plugs, and remove the tool box cover.
3. Draw the snap connector cluster out of the frame aperture, and release the connectors so that those on the engine are free from the main wiring loom.
4. Then unscrew the carburettor's mixing chamber top, and pull out the slide assembly. Fix this to the frame with tape, so that it cannot be damaged. Alternatively, remove it from the cable.
5. Next, loosen the screw which secures the air cleaner hose to the carburettor intake, and undo the two 6 mm nuts which hold the carburettor to the intake port flange. The carburettor can then be detached.
6. From the underside of the machine, take the four 8 mm bolts which secure the footrest bar to the crankcase. If it is proposed to work on the bottom end of the unit, this is the time to drain the oil too. The drain plug is located centrally in the bottom of the case.
7. To free the driving chain, and the clutch cable, the left rear crankcase cover must be detached. This is secured by 6 mm cross-headed screws, which may be very tight. The best tool to use here is an impact screwdriver. Without one, you may have to rely upon jarring the threads with sharp blows from a hammer, interposing a soft-metal drift to avoid damage. Don't overdo things, or you may all too easily crack the light alloy cover. Really tenacious screws can often be shifted by heating the alloy with rags wrung out in very hot water.
8. Once the cover is off, free the clutch cable from the short operating arm.

9 Then turn the rear wheel until the spring link on the driving chain is just behind the engine sprocket. Break the chain at this point, attaching wire loops to each end so that it does not coil up inside the chain case.
10 On the other side of the machine, detach the brake pedal return spring and the stop lamp operating spring.
11 Then remove the silencer mounting nuts, undo the pipes at the cylinder head flange, and lift both assemblies away.
12 Place wooden blocks or a stout wooden box under the engine, to act as a support. Then undo the four engine mounting nuts—two at the top, where the unit mates with the frame bracket; two at the rear of the gearbox—and the engine is free to be lifted away to the bench.

Removing the Cylinder Head

1 From the top of the unit, remove the eight 8 mm blind nuts and the single 6 mm bolt which secure the cylinder head cover. This can be then lifted off.
2 Now the cam chain must be freed. Take out the sparking plugs, and operate the kickstarter pedal gently so that the spring link on the cam chain comes to the top of the sprocket. Carefully detach the spring link, having first slipped loops of wire through the adjacent links so that the "broken" chain cannot slip down the cam chain tunnel into the bottom of the crankcase.
3 The head can now be lifted off the studs. If it jams, jar it gently with a block of softwood. But take care not to damage the fins.

Decarbonizing

The procedure for decarbonizing this unit is precisely the same as that outlined on page 35.

Cylinder Barrel Removal

1 From the rear of the cam chain tunnel, remove the single 6 mm bolt which holds the casting to the crankcase.
2 The cylinder block can then be lifted away. Take due care not to allow the pistons to fall against other parts of the unit as this is done, or their working surfaces may be damaged.

Piston Removal

1 The gudgeon-pins are located by circlips, in the normal way. Ease the circlips out of their grooves—again, taking care not to drop them into the crankcase.
2 Press out the gudgeon-pins. If they are tight, expand the pistons by applying rags wrung out in very hot water.

WORKING ON THE 175 C.C. UNIT 55

Do not transpose pistons between the two bores. Each must be reassembled into its original cylinder.

Reassembly

Apart from resetting the valve timing, reassembly after a decoke is a simple reversal of the stripping procedure. It is important to note, however, that if the cam chain tensioner push bar is not first pressed fully home into its housing in the head, and temporarily locked with the adjuster bolt, the cam chain cannot be reconnected.

1 Set the pistons to T.D.C., and feed the cam chain through the tunnel as the head is offered up.
2 With the marked tooth on the camshaft sprocket uppermost, reconnect the timing chain.
3 Refit the cylinder head cover and tighten the head nuts in the correct sequence. Preferably, they should be torqued to 11·6–15·2 lb. ft.
4 Next, re-tension the timing chain in the normal way.
5 Reset the tappet clearances.
6 Replace the tappet covers. The engine can then be installed in the frame.

Stripping the Bottom End

For a major overhaul, proceed to the stage of removing the cylinder head, as already detailed, but in addition detach the right and left crankcase covers.

1 On the left-hand side, first detach the generator cover plate, undo the centre bolt of the A.C. generator's rotor and, using a puller, draw the rotor off the shaft.
2 Then remove the cross-headed screws which secure the crankcase cover, and pull it away complete with the generator stator. Note that the rotor is keyed to the crankshaft. Take care not to lose this key during dismantling.
3 Turning, now, to the right-hand side of the unit take off the crankcase cover. This entails removing the kickstarter and the ten cross-headed screws which hold the cover to the crankcase. Note that two of these—one at the front, below the oil filter; one at the rear, above the kickstarter—are longer than the rest.
4 Dismantle the oil filter by pulling off its cap, flattening the internal lock washer, and undoing the mounting nut.
5 Strip the clutch by releasing its four pressure plate retaining bolts and withdrawing the springs and plates, and the operating thrust button. Then spring open the 20 mm circlip which holds the clutch centre to the shaft. Do not attempt to draw the unit off the engine yet, since it is still held by the oil pump. The nuts

holding this pump to the crankcase must first be detached, and then the clutch and pump can be drawn away as one unit.

6 Now remove the 8 mm nut from the stud beside the oil filter orifice and the 6 mm nut from the stud above the kickstarter spindle, and invert the partially-stripped engine.

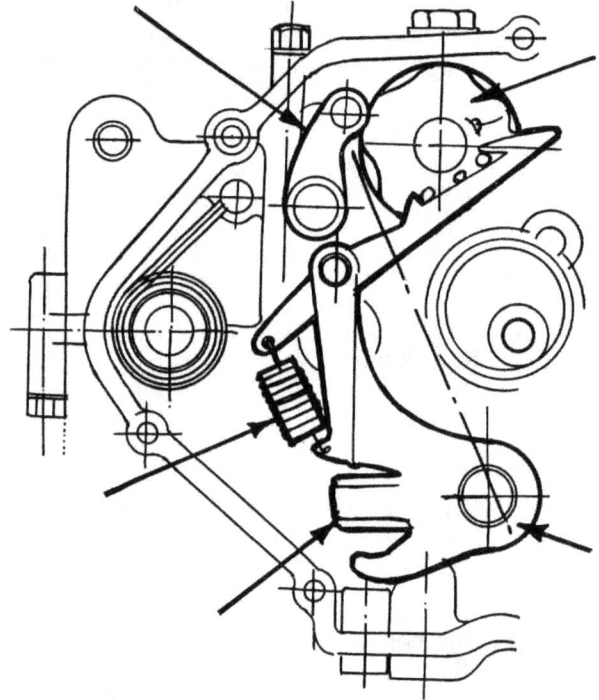

Fig. 25. When assembling the 175 c.c. gearbox, use this diagram to ensure that your selector mechanism is correct. The arrowed components must be in the positions as shown here

7 Detach the peripheral 6 mm and 8 mm bolts and the single 8 mm nut from the lower crankcase.
8 Where a starter motor is fitted (it is not standard for all countries) remove its mounting bolts from the right of the crankcase and the single supporting bolt on the left-hand side, and detach the motor.
9 Keeping the gearshift arm disengaged from the gearshift drum, the lower section of the crankcase can now be drawn away from the upper, leaving the crankshaft and transmission shafts in place. The crankshaft can be lifted out, as can the main and layshafts, leaving only the selector mechanisms and the cam chain tensioner in the case.

WORKING ON THE 175 C.C. UNIT

10 The tensioner is secured by two 6 mm bolts set between the two cylinders. After removing these the tensioner can be lifted away.

It will not normally be either necessary or desirable to strip the gear selector mechanism, but the procedure is fairly straightforward—

1 First, flatten the locking tabs on the guide pin on each selector fork and undo the pins. They are hexagon-headed.
2 Remove the neutral-indicator switch from the end of the selector drum, remove the pivot bolt from the stop arm, and remove the arm and its plate.
3 The selector drum can then be drawn out. In the lower case, the gear selector spindle is held by a circlip.

The Kickstarter

Normally, this mechanism would not have been disturbed during dismantling. It is located immediately to the rear of the transmission gear train, and operates through it. It can be removed by splitting the cases and lifting the complete kickstarter shaft assembly away, just as in the case of the transmission shafts. To strip it—

1 Slide the return spring from the free end of the shaft.
2 From the left side, remove the circlip which secures the friction spring and the starter pinion. The pinion can then be detached.

Reassembly involves reversing the stripping sequence.

Engine Reassembly

In general, simply reverse the stripping procedure and the unit will not be difficult to reassemble. Note that when refitting the selector mechanism, the selector spindle is entered from the right side of the lower case. The sequence is—

1 Fit the selector drum.
2 Fit the selector forks.
3 Fit the neutral indicator switch.
4 Refit the selector drum stop arm to complete reassembly in the upper case, so far as the selector mechanism is concerned. In the lower case, refit the gear-change return spring, and offer up the gear selector spindle from the right-hand side.

10 Working on the 250/305 c.c. units

AMONG the most popular machines Hondas have ever made are the sports versions of the 250 and 305 c.c. motor-cycles—the business-like CB.72 and CB.77. However, the touring versions, for all their unfamiliar Oriental angularity, also had an appeal to the market.

The engines are basically similar, although the frames are entirely different in concept and construction.

Engine Removal: Models C.72 and C.77

1 Remove the left exhaust system.
2 Detach the left footrest and gear pedal.
3 Take off the left carburettor shield and pull off the vent tube from the head.
4 Detach the left plug cap, the carburettor flange nut, and the breather pipe.
5 Undo the left upper rear engine mounting bolt, located in front of and above the rear fork pivot.
6 Detach the right exhaust system and the right footrest.
7 Detach the starter motor cable from the solenoid switch.
8 Remove the right dust shield and the right engine cover.
9 Release the clutch cable from the arm on the inside of the cover.
10 Break the chain at the connecting link.
11 Disconnect the wiring at the snap connectors.
12 Remove the right plug cap and air-vent tube.
13 Detach the remaining carburettor flange nut.
14 Remove the upper engine mounting bolt from the cylinder head mounting point.
15 Remove the last engine mounting bolt at the rear, and drop the engine from the frame.

Engine Removal: Models CB.72 and CB.77

1 Detach the dual seat by removing the two rear mounting bolts and sliding the seat from its front mounting.

2 Remove the rear mounting bolt from the fuel tank. Detach the fuel pipes.
3 Detach the left footrest and gear-change assembly.
4 Remove the left exhaust system.
5 Release the crankcase well-cover.

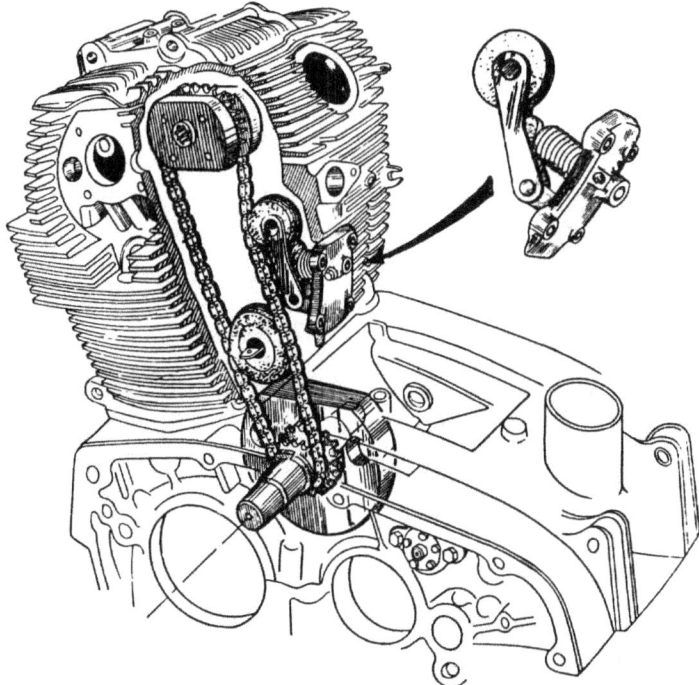

Fig. 26. On the 250 c.c. machines—and on the 305 c.c. derivants—this is how the tensioner is arranged. In these machines, the cam chain operates in a tunnel cast into the block and head between the two working cylinders

6 Free the rev-counter cable from the drive on the cylinder head.
7 Take off the air-filter cover and disconnect the battery.
8 Free the starter motor cable from the solenoid.
9 Detach air filter hoses and the throttle cables.
10 Loosen all engine mounting bolts by releasing the nuts.
11 On the right side, detach the brake pedal, footrest, and stop light switch.
12 Detach the right exhaust system.
13 Remove the dynamo cover and the right crankcase cover.
14 Disconnect the clutch cable at the cover end and take off the drive chain connecting link.

15 Disconnect the engine wiring at the snap connectors.
16 Remove the upper mounting bolt, followed by the rear mounting bolts, and drop the engine out of the frame.

Head Removal: Models C.72, C.77, CB.72, and CB.77

1 Detach the condenser, followed by the eight cylinder head nuts.
2 Remove the cam chain tensioner from the rear of the cylinder block and take out the sparking plugs.
3 Turn the crankshaft until the cam chain connecting link is at the top of the camshaft sprocket, projecting through the cylinder head. Remove the link. Take care not to drop it into the tunnel. It is also advisable to loop wire through each free end of the chain to secure it.
4 Lift the cylinder head from its studs.

Removal of Valve Gear: C.72, C.77, CB.72, CB.77

1 Remove the valve caps, the contact-breaker assembly, and the left cylinder head cover.
2 Loosen all tappet-adjusting screws.
3 Swing each rocker in turn out of the way and insert a Honda valve spring compressor tool. Compress the spring and, using thin-nosed pliers, lift out the collets. As each valve is removed mark it to ensure that it is refitted correctly, in its original place.

Replacing Head and Re-timing: Models C.72, C.77, CB.72, and CB.77

1 Re-insert all valves.
2 Slide the cylinder head on to its studs and, with the aid of the securing wires, feed the cam chain through the head tunnel and round the sprocket.
3 Refit the head nuts. For the purposes of identification these can be thought of as being numbered in this way, as seen from the saddle: front, left to right, Nos. 6, 2, 4, 8. Rear, left to right, Nos. 7, 3, 1, 5. Of these, Nos. 1, 2, 3, 4 are white nuts and Nos. 5, 6, 7, 8 are tinged yellow. Screw all nuts finger tight at first. Then lock them fully home, two or three threads at a time, working from nut to nut in the correct numerical sequence.
4 To re-time the engine, turn the crankshaft until the "T" mark on the alternator rotor is in line with the arrow mark on the crankcase. Then bring the camshaft sprocket tooth which is marked with a punch dot on to the exact centre line of the cylinder. Refit the chain, making certain that the open end of the spring link points to the *rear* of the engine.

WORKING ON THE 250/305 C.C. UNITS 61

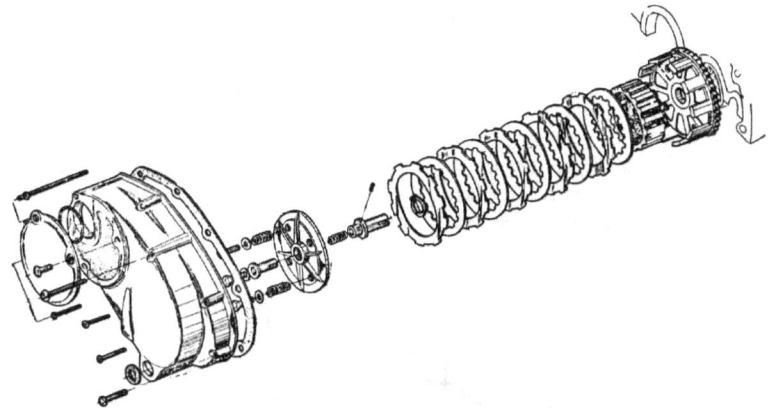

Fig. 27. An exploded view of the clutch on the 250 and 305 c.c. sports twin Hondas

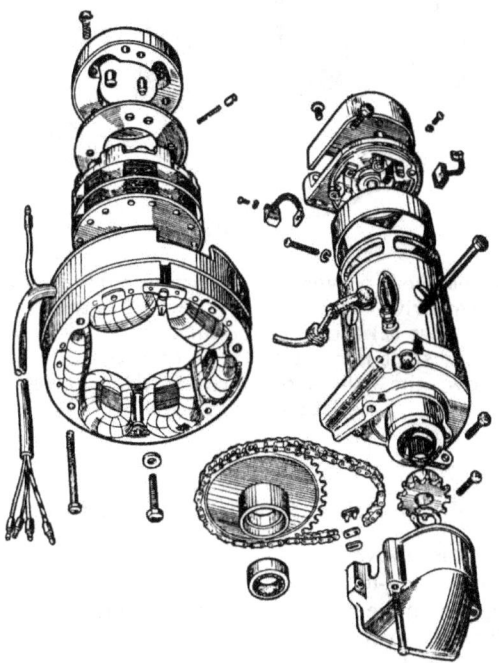

Fig. 28. The layout of the starter motor and alternator employed on the standard and sports machines in the 250/305 c.c. ranges

Clutch Removal: Models C.72, C.77, CB.72, and CB.77

1 Remove the left crankcase cover and detach the oil filter and drive.
2 Free the tab washer and remove the crankshaft centre nut.
3 Detach the four 10 mm bolts on the clutch pressure plate.
4 Remove the thrust button.
5 With circlip pliers spring out the 25 mm circlip on the main shaft.
6 Lift out the clutch plates and the clutch centre. Note the order of the plates for subsequent reassembly.

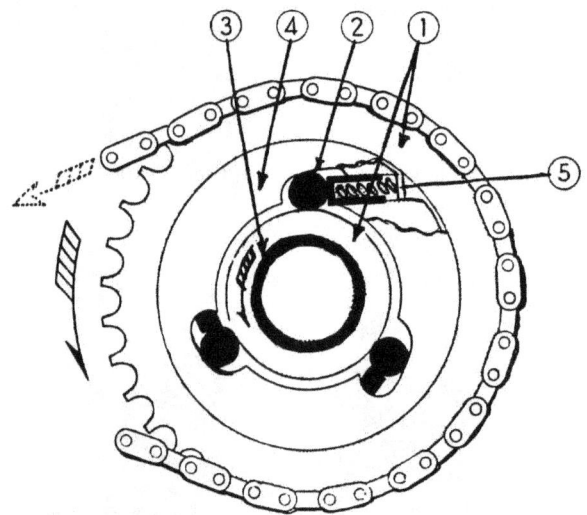

Fig. 29. This freewheel prevents the starter motor being driven by the engine. When the driven sprocket (1) is rotated in the direction shown by the arrow the rollers (2) are forced against the crankshaft and so turn it. But as soon as the shaft is rotating faster than the drive sprocket centrifugal force throws the rollers outwards in their guides (4) against the resistance of springs (5)

Clutch Reassembly: Models C.72, C.77, CB.72, and CB.77

Merely reverse the above order. When doing so, however, check the operation of the spring-loaded oil conduit. On installation of the clutch pressure plate, tighten the bolts a few threads at a time, working diagonally from one bolt to the next.

Use a new tab washer on the crankshaft sprocket, and when installing the crankcase cover be careful that it does not foul the pin on the oil filter shaft.

Stripping the Gearbox

Once the crankcase has been split—which simply involves inverting the engine and removing the 15 peripheral nuts and bolts—it is an easy job to lift away the lower crankcase half. This leaves the crankshaft, the main and layshafts, and the kickstarter spindle in the upper case, from which they are simply lifted.

As with the 125 and 150 c.c. models, circlips are used to retain certain of the gears on their shafts; and the selector drum mechanism remains in the upper case. It will not normally be necessary to withdraw this, but where this is required the general principles set out under the CB.92 section can be applied.

Reassembly, again, involves reversing the dismantling sequence. Note, however, that Honda advise the use of a sealing compound between the two crankcase halves and that great care must be taken, when applying this, not to allow it to block oil holes.

11 Working on the 450 c.c. unit

WITHOUT any doubt whatsoever the massive 450 c.c. power unit is the most complicated of the Honda engines, and it is essential to possess a number of special tools before any work at all can be done on it, so far as dismantling is concerned.

This point is of vital importance. You *must* have available the special Honda tool for unriveting the endless cam chain and the special tool for installing the new link. You should ideally also possess a torque wrench—and you definitely need the special adaptor required for fitting a torque or ratchet wrench to the torsion bars which replace valve springs on this unit. Without this equipment—which may set you back somewhere in the region of £30 or so to purchase—you cannot even lift the cylinder head to carry out an ordinary decoke. So, if you haven't got it, don't attempt it. You run the grave risk of wrecking your engine if you do—and a new engine will cost even more than the tools! Unless you plan to do a great deal of maintenance—or can persuade a Honda dealer to hire you the necessary tools against a deposit—you would be better advised to leave all but routine work on this unit to a fully-equipped workshop.

Removing the Engine

Where the requisite tools are available, overhauling begins with the removal of the engine from the frame. Turn off the petrol, remove the fuel leads, lift the dual seat, and undo the tank retaining bolt. Take off the fuel tank, and then follow this sequence—

1 Detach the throttle control cables.
2 Remove the air cleaner covers, and detach the elements.
3 Take off the carburettors.
4 Remove the exhaust pipes and silencers.
5 At the engine end, detach the clutch control cable.
6 Detach the left-hand footrest and the gear pedal and take off the rear half of the left-hand crankcase cover.
7 Break the final drive chain at its spring link and remove the chain.
8 Unplug the cable snap connector cluster beside the saddle tube and the leads to the contact-breaker in the cylinder head.
9 Remove the plug caps.

10 Detach the starter cable from its connection under the dual seat, having first displaced its terminal cover.
11 Release the rev. counter cable from its connection on the right-hand side of the cylinder head.
12 Remove the engine bolts—four 10 mm bolts on the front engine plate; two 10 mm bolts at the bottom of the engine at the rear; three 8 mm bolts on the rear engine plate; four 8 mm bolts on the cylinder head upper mounting plate—and draw the engine out to the left.

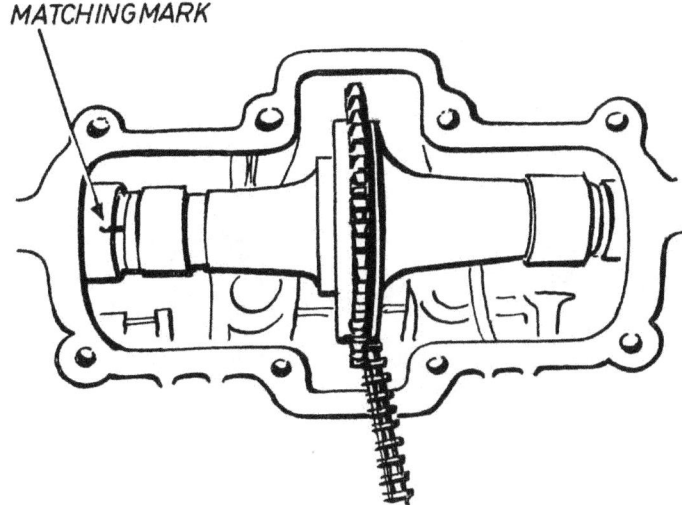

Fig. 30. How the timing marks on the camshaft and cylinder head must be aligned when re-timing the valves on the 450

Head Removal

Start by cleaning the unit thoroughly, as described on page 37. Then remove the head by following this procedure—

1 Take off both inlet and exhaust side tappet covers, and remove the spark plugs.
2 Working from the inlet side, turn the engine until the special link on the cam chain is actually on the inlet camshaft sprocket. You will readily recognize this link, since it is of a lighter colour than the rest. It has pins of a softer material to aid riveting and un-riveting. Slip thin wire through the ends of the chain to locate it while dismantling is in progress.
3 Remove the eight 10 mm dome nuts which hold the head, working in the reverse order to the tightening sequence to avoid distortion. The head can then be lifted.

4 On the inlet side, remove the lock-nuts of the left-hand and right-hand cam follower spindles. Then take off both side covers and take out the camshaft.
5 On the exhaust side, detach the right-hand lock-nut and take off the rev. counter gearbox. On the left of the engine, remove the contact-breaker points cover and undo the left-hand lock-nut.
6 Undo the screws holding the contact-breaker, and take off the complete unit. Underneath it is the centrifugal advance/retard mechanism. This must also be detached. Then remove the

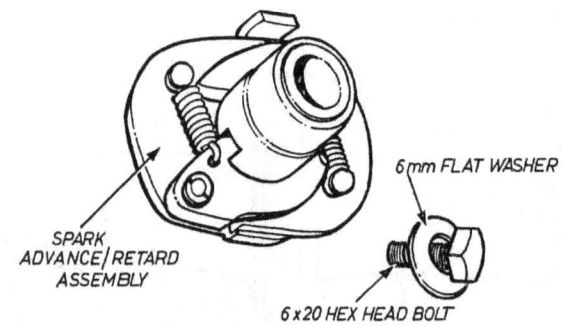

Fig. 31. A centrifugal advance/retard mechanism is generally employed. This example is from the 450.

contact-breaker points housing and withdraw the exhaust camshaft.
7 Using the special adaptor, apply pressure in the direction indicated by the arrow stamped on the face of the torsion bar which acts as a valve spring in this engine. By keeping up the pressure you relieve the locating bolt of load, and this can be undone and removed. The torsion bar assembly can then be detached from the head. Repeat this for each of the four bars. The valve-operating arms and the valves can then be demounted.
8 Decarbonize as described in Chapter 6.
9 Reverse the general sequence to reassemble the head, making sure that each valve assembly is kept complete and not mixed up with parts from any of the others. Each torsion bar, complete with outer case and holder, must be assembled with the torsion bar direction mark on the holder side. Offer the bar up and feed it through the splined valve-operating arm. These components are so manufactured that they will fit only in one position.
10 Replace the valve. Its collets must seat properly both on the valve stem and on the valve operating arm. Remember, too, to check the oil seal atop the valve guide. If this is worn or damaged, oil will

be allowed to enter the combustion chamber, leading to reduced performance and heavy carbon formation.
11 Fix the special adaptor to your wrench and link it to the torsion bar. The bar must now be turned in the direction of the arrow (until it is tightened, preferably, to a torque of 9 lb. ft. or until the locating bolt can be inserted and tightened. The same operation is performed with all the remaining valves.

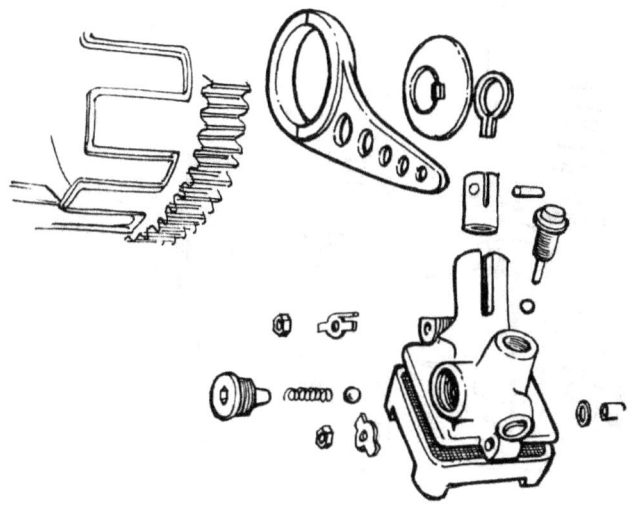

Fig. 32. The oil pump of the 450 c.c. model shown in exploded form

12 Now the cam followers and spindles on the inlet side can be replaced. Offer up the inlet camshaft, with the oil pick-up on the right-hand side, and then instal both right-hand and left-hand covers. The spindle lock-nut should be temporarily tightened.
13 Instal the exhaust side cam followers, spindles, and camshaft. Match up the rev. counter gearbox pinion with the camshaft groove, and on the other side refit the points housing, the advance/retard mechanism and the contact-breaker assembly. Then take the lock-nut up to finger-tightness.
14 Check that the camshafts revolve easily. There should be 0·003/0·014 in. (0·5–0·35 mm play). Adjust this with shims if necessary.
15 Fit the three guide sleeves, two stud gaskets and a new head gasket on to the cylinder and offer up the head. Using the wires attached to its ends, feed the camshaft chain through its tunnel.
16 With the head reseated, the two right-hand cylinder studs must be fitted with copper washers. On the other six studs, special flat

washers are used. The domed nuts are then tightened down, in the sequence shown, to a torque of 25·3 lb. ft. (3·5 kg. m.).

17 Each camshaft has a line marked on its right-hand side. This must be aligned with the line scribed on each of the shaft bearing housings. The crankshaft is then rotated until the alternator

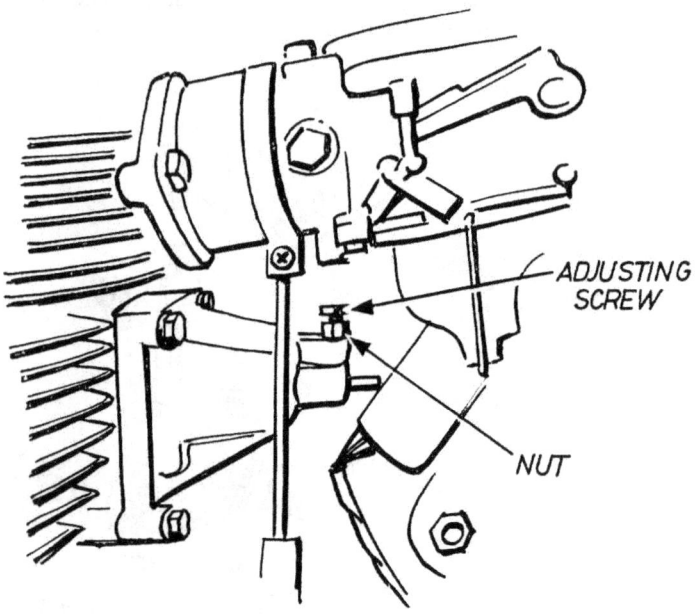

Fig. 33. The cam chain tensioner on the 450 is adjusted by setting the generator rotor's "LT" mark against the crankcase index mark and loosening the lock-nut on the adjuster. The adjuster bolt is then loosened and spring pressure forces the tensioner harder against the chain. Re-tighten the bolt to hold the new adjustment and do up the lock-nut. The same method is used on all models except the 125 and 150 c.c. machines. These have a crankcase-mounted adjuster

rotor mark "LT" is in line with the index mark which you will find at "10 o'clock" on the stator housing. While this is being done, keep hold of the wires on the camshaft chain so that it is not pulled into the tunnel.

18 While the LT mark is aligned with the pointer, check that the camshafts have not moved. Then thread the chain on to the sprockets so that its ends fall on the inlet camshaft sprocket, and again check that all three marks are properly aligned. Insert the special link—a new one, of course—and rivet it into place with the correct service tool.

19 Loosen the lock-nut on the cam chain adjuster and loosen the adjuster bolt. Immediately re-tighten the bolt, and lock the nut firmly.

20 Reset the valve clearances on the left-hand cylinder—still with the LT mark against the index—so that the clearance between the cam and the cam follower is 0·001 in. (0·03 mm). To adjust this, loosen the cam follower spindle lock-nut and turn it, with a screwdriver, inwards to increase the clearance or outwards to decrease it. Hold the spindle steady, re-tighten the lock-nut, and check the gap once more. On the right-hand cylinder the same procedure is adopted, save that the rotor must be turned through 180° so that the "T" mark is aligned with the index pointer. Whenever the tappets are adjusted the engine must be stone cold, and both valves on the cylinder in question must be closed, with the piston at top dead centre. Overtight valves must be avoided at all costs.

21 Check the ignition timing by turning the engine until the contact-breaker points are fully open. Set the gap to 0·012–0·016 in. (0·3–0·4 mm) and align the LF mark on the rotor with the stator index pointer. The points should just be opening—a setting best checked with a test lamp linked to the contacts and to earth. If adjustment is required, loosen the two clamping screws which hold the contact-breaker plate assembly and turn it until the points begin to break. Then lock the plate. Turn the rotor anti-clockwise to bring the "F" mark against the pointer. If the points have not started to open here, reset the gap at this point to 0·0015 in.— roughly the thickness of a cigarette paper. If the gap is wider than this, reduce it.

Cylinder Removal

Once the engine has been demounted from the frame and the head has been removed, lifting the cylinder itself involves nothing more than raising it clear of its studs. Do not let the pistons fall against the unit. Set them so that they are at an equal height in their respective cylinders, and support them as they emerge. Detach the gudgeon-pin circlips, press out the pins, and place each piston inside its own cylinder for safe keeping.

Clutch Removal

Drain the oil from the unit and remove the kickstarter and the right-hand crankcase cover. Then follow this procedure—

1 Detach the 6 mm bolt which holds the oil filter cap. Then insert an 8 mm bolt and use this as a puller to release the cap. Flatten the locking washer, undo the 16 mm nut inside the rotor, and pull the filter body away from the engine.

2 Undo the six 6 mm bolts on the clutch pressure plate, and draw out the plates and springs. Besides the pressure plate itself there are seven plain plates and seven friction plates.

3 Detach the 25 mm circlip in the clutch centre, having removed the mushroom-headed thrust member, and draw out the clutch centre hub.

4 Flatten the locking washer and remove the bolt which secures the oil pump. Then lift off the clutch drum and the pump as one unit. When rebuilding the unit, simply reverse this order.

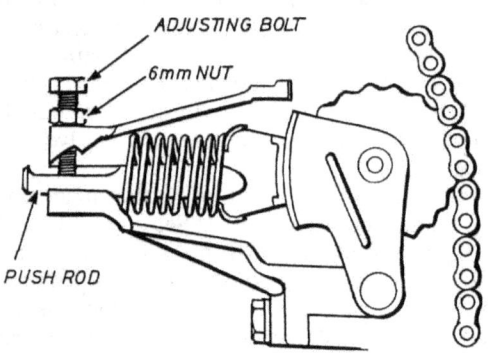

Fig. 34. The 450's cam chain tensioner in detail, showing the spring and the adjuster mechanism

Oil Pump Condition

Check the condition of the oil pump as described on page 51.

Splitting the Crankcase

Drain the oil and remove the engine from the frame. Remove the cylinder head, the cylinder, the right-hand crankcase cover, the oil pump and clutch. Remove the neutral switch from the left-hand side of the crankcase and free the clamp holding the alternator leads. Take off the left-hand crankcase cover, complete with the stator, and remove the starter motor and the generator rotor. Draw off the starter sprocket and chain, having removed the starter sprocket set plate, which is held by a single bolt. Then undo the two bolts which hold the final drive sprocket. The work then proceeds thus—

1 Detach the circlip on the left-hand side and withdraw the gear lever spindle. The selector arm will come away with it.

2 On the upper side of the crankcase are four nuts. Detach these, and then turn the unit over. Underneath, you will find nine nuts.

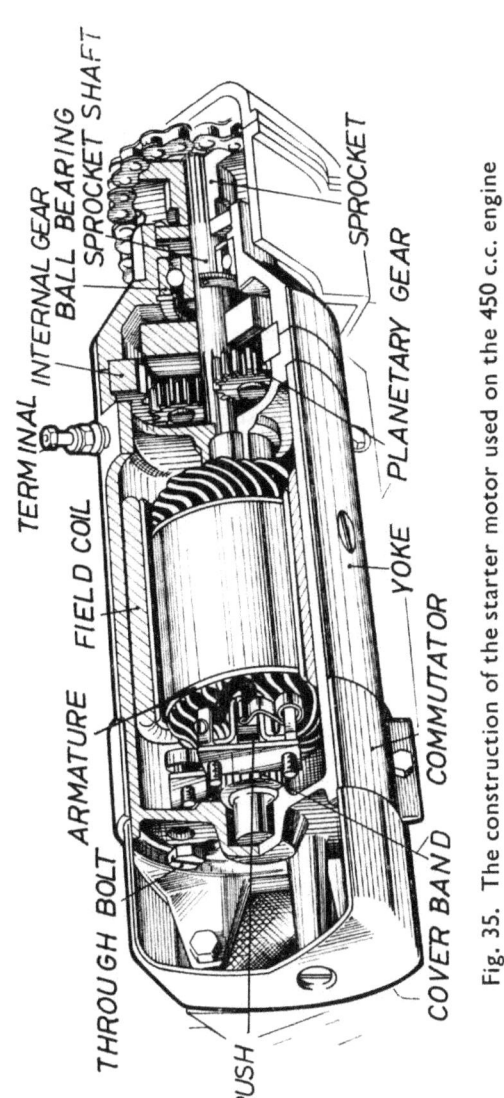

Fig. 35. The construction of the starter motor used on the 450 c.c. engine

When these are detached the lower half of the crankcase can be lifted off.

3 Draw out the camshaft chain, and then undo the eight nuts on the bearing housings. The crankshaft can then be lifted as a unit.

4 The gear shafts are also simply lifted from their place in the upper half of the casing. The gear shift drum stop should then be unscrewed from the right-hand side of the gearcase; the fork guide pins pulled out; and the drum guide bolt removed. The drum itself will then come away.

5 The kickstarter mechanism is contained in the lower half of the case. It is dismantled by removing its spring, and taking out the 25 mm circlip and the 8 mm bolt which secure the kickstarter shaft.

6 Reassemble all mechanisms in the reverse order to that employed for dismantling, taking especial care to take up all bolts evenly. Use a smear of non-setting jointing compound on the crankcase joints as an insurance against oil leaks.

12 Honda Carburettors

ALTHOUGH the 450 c.c. models employ a constant-vacuum carburettor of a design unfamiliar to motor-cyclists—though car owners would not find it unusual—most of the twins are fitted with conventional needle-jet instruments, of which the pattern fitted to the 160 c.c. models can be taken as typical. It comprises a spring-loaded throttle slide, raised by a cable, to which is attached a tapered needle. This operates in a jet, partly immersed in the fuel contained in the float chamber, whose lower end carries the main jet. An air bleed into the needle jet aids emulsifying of the fuel for easier mixing. As the slide is raised more and more air enters the venturi of the carburettor, and the needle progressively permits more fuel to pass through the needle jet into the air stream. For slow running, with the throttle closed, a separate slow-running jet meters a small amount of emulsified fuel into the venturi. The fuel level in the float chamber is maintained by a conventional float and needle valve arrangement, the valve cutting off the flow of fuel when the float reaches a pre-determined level. To prevent over-flooding, a drain tube allows excess petrol to flow out of the chamber, just like the overflow pipe on a domestic cistern. An extra-rich mixture for starting is obtained by reducing the air supply by means of a choke valve in the intake.

On the sports machines, there is also a power jet system which feeds an extra supply of fuel into the intake at very high engine speeds.

Low-speed Adjustment. Before carrying out carburettor adjustments, ensure that the machine's tappets are properly set; the timing is correct; the contact-breaker is properly gapped; and the plugs are clean and their gaps correct. The unit must also be brought up to operating temperature.

Set the throttle stop screw (or screws, in the case of multiple-carburettor installations) to obtain an idling speed of 1,000/1,200 r.p.m. Then turn the air screw/s a quarter of a turn at a time, in or out, until the engine speeds up. At this point, the throttle stop/s must be readjusted to restore the correct idling speed.

Now repeat the sequence, until a setting is found at which the idling is steady. Check that the engine does not hesitate or tend to cut out when the throttle is opened.

Then check the adjustment of the throttle cable/s. This is done with

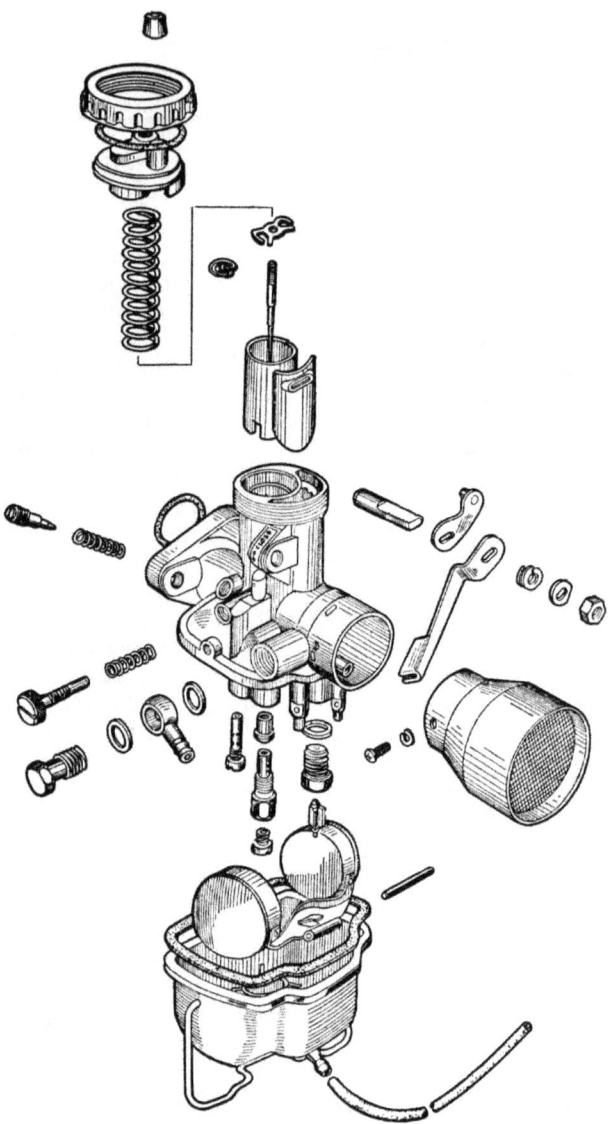

Fig. 36. An exploded view of the carburettor of the 150 c.c. C.92 twin

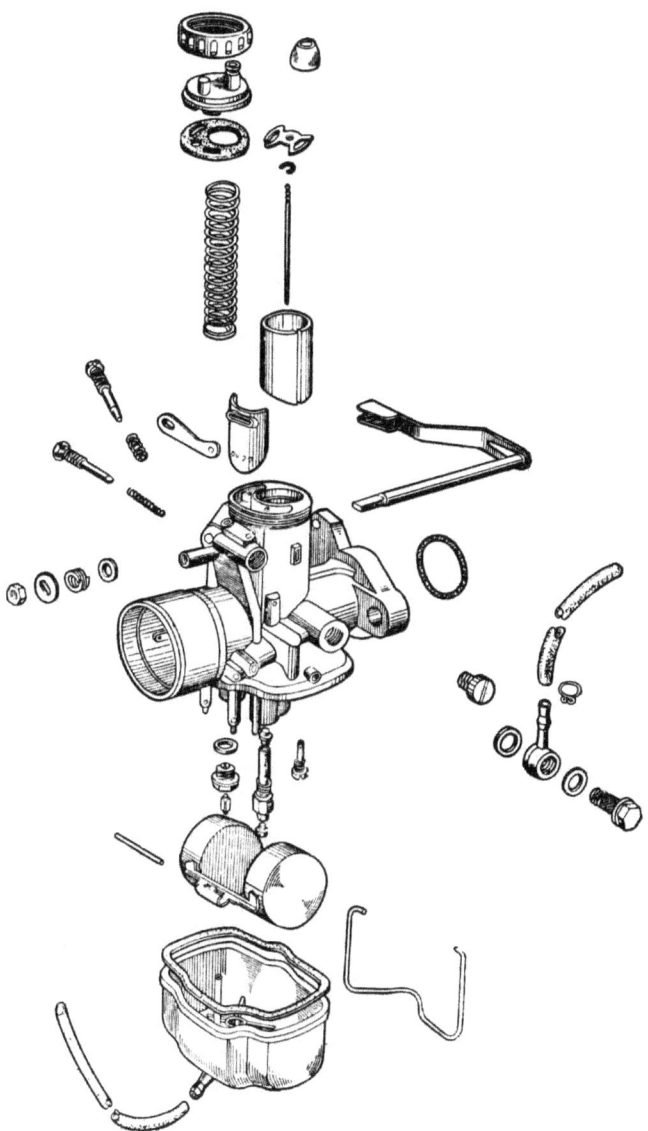

Fig. 37. The carburettor used on the C.72 250 c.c. twin

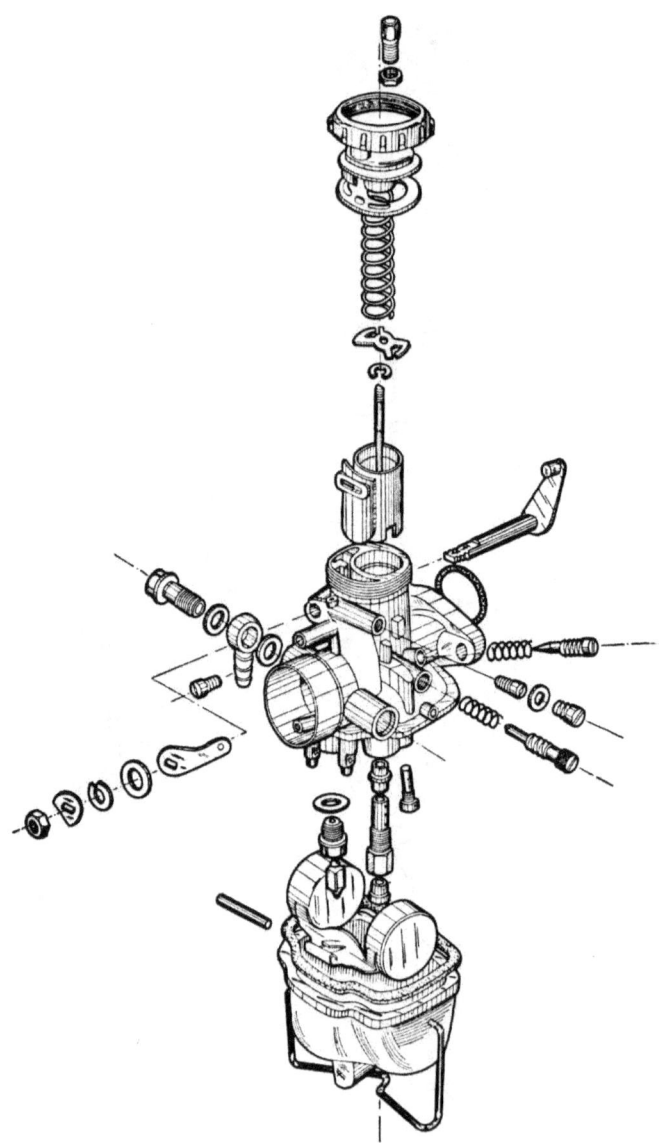

Fig. 38. The CB.72 250 c.c. sports twin uses two of these instruments

the threaded adjuster at the top of each carburettor. Turning the adjuster to the left takes up play, and to the right increases it.

Adjustment in the Mid-speed Range. The air-screw/throttle stop combination covers the running range up to one-eighth of the throttle opening. From there to half throttle, the decisive factors are the position of the tapered needle relative to the needle jet, and the amount of cut-away on the slide. Although it is possible to use different slides, in practice adjustment in this speed range is confined to raising or lowering the needle, which is held by means of a spring clip. The higher the needle is raised, the richer the mixture becomes. Conversely, lowering the needle weakens the mixture.

A rich mixture is indicated by the emission of black smoke from the exhaust at moderate speeds, and by sooting-up of the plugs. If this occurs, the mixing chamber top is unscrewed and the throttle slide is drawn out. It is detached from the cable by compressing the spring and pressing the cable nipple out of its seating in the slide. The needle is then removed —a note having first been made of which groove is engaged by the clip— and replaced with the clip one groove higher—i.e., towards the blunt end of the needle.

Where the mixture is too weak (rough running during engine braking, etc.) the needle is lifted by one notch instead. This means setting the clip one groove *lower*.

High-speed Adjustment. Above half-throttle, adjustment must be made by fitting a different main jet. The existing one may be either too large— allowing too much fuel to pass—or too small, in which case it will starve the engine. Or, of course, it may be just the right size . . .

To check, run the machine at full throttle and slightly close the choke valve. If the machine immediately slows down the main jet is either the right one or else it is too large, and only a substitution test will tell you which. It is easy enough to do. Just unclip the float chamber, unscrew the existing main jet, and screw in a smaller one in its place.

If, when the choke test is made, the speed actually increases you have too small a main jet. Restricting the air flow by operating the choke therefore restores the correct air/fuel balance and the engine runs better. Again, take out the existing main jet and fit a larger one. You will have to test and re-test until you hit on the right one for your particular machine. But don't be haphazard about it. Work with jets one stage larger or smaller at a time.

THE CONSTANT-VACUUM CARBURETTOR

Superficially, the constant-vacuum carburettor fitted to the 450 c.c. Honda is similar to the needle-jet instruments used on the smaller machines. Like them, it has a throttle slide carrying a needle which operates in a submerged needle jet, with a main jet on the end. However, the slide and needle are

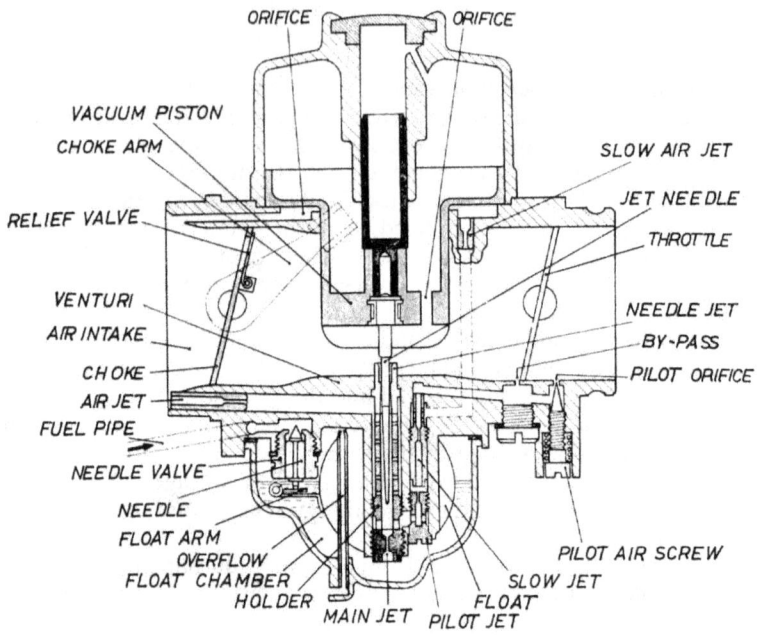

Fig. 39. The constant-vacuum carburettor employed on the 450 c.c. models will be unfamiliar to most motor-cyclists, although it is widely employed on cars

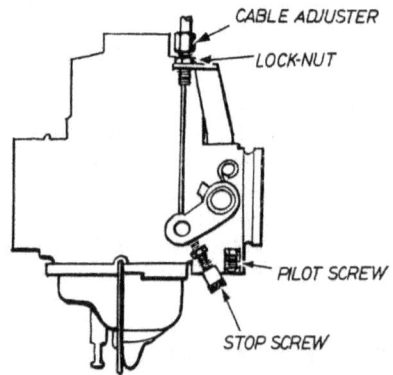

Fig. 40. Although it may look complicated, these are the only points on the constant-vacuum carburettor which will normally be adjusted

controlled by engine vacuum, not by a throttle cable. And to vary the engine speed a butterfly throttle is used.

With the engine stopped, the throttle slide—which is mounted on a piston—drops by its own weight until it and the needle are in their lowest position. Under these conditions the pressure acting on the underside of the piston (through an air inlet in the main intake) and on the upper face of the piston (through a drilling in the piston) are equal.

When the engine is started, the upper face of the piston is subjected to the vacuum in the venturi, while the under face is influenced by the higher pressure of the air in the intake. Therefore, the piston rises, lifting the slide and needle and so controlling the vacuum and the rate of fuel flow through the needle jet. When the unit is running at full speed the slide is fully raised. As with the conventional carburettors, there is a subsidiary jet for slow running.

Slow-running Adjustment. Follow the procedure set out on page 73 until an idling speed of 1,200 r.p.m. is obtained.

Cruising-speed Adjustment. The only adjustment which is possible here is to vary the size of the slow-running jet, which is set above the pilot jet in the float chamber.

Medium-speed Adjustment. As with the conventional carburettor, the mixture setting in the medium-speed range is altered by raising or lowering the throttle needle. This cannot be done by the private owner.

High-speed Adjustment. Here, again, the only adjustment possible is to alter the size of the main jet. Follow the general working instructions given on page 77.

13 Suspension and Brakes

THERE are only two basic types of suspension employed on the Honda twins—the combination of swinging-fork rear springing with telescopic front forks on the CB.160, the CB.72 and CB.77, the CD.175 and the CB.450; and swinging-fork rear with leading-link front forks on the earlier Benley 125 and 150 c.c. machines, the C.72 and the C.77. In each case, the construction of the front forks is so similar that the same set of working instructions can be adapted to any machine in the group.

Telescopic Front Forks

The following dismantling sequence applies to the CB.450, and can be used for any other machine in the Honda range with telescopic forks. To remove the actual fork legs does not require disturbance of the upper fork section comprising the steering head and upper and lower bridges. Preliminary work involves blocking up the machine under the crankcase to bring the front wheel clear of the ground. Then follow this sequence—

1 Disconnect the speedometer drive and the front brake cable.
2 Flatten the tab washer on the bolt securing the front brake torque arm to the brake back-plate and remove the bolt.
3 Detach the two 8 mm nuts at the bottom of each fork leg and drop out the wheel by removing the lower clamps.
4 Take off the front mudguard by freeing the two 6 mm bolts holding its stays to each fork leg, and the 8 mm bolts on the U-shaped upper support.
5 Loosen the 10 mm clamp bolt on each side of the lower fork bridge.
6 Undo the chromium-plated top fork bolt which holds each leg to the upper bridge.
7 Pull each leg smartly downwards to free it from the machine.
8 Drain out the oil, either through the drain plug set in the lower part of each leg or by inverting the leg itself.
9 Using the special peg spanner, unscrew the front fork seal housing and separate the lower slider from the fork leg.
10 Take out the two springs from each leg. They are coupled together, and the lower spring is the longer of the two.
11 The damper mechanism is fixed to the bottom of the fork leg.

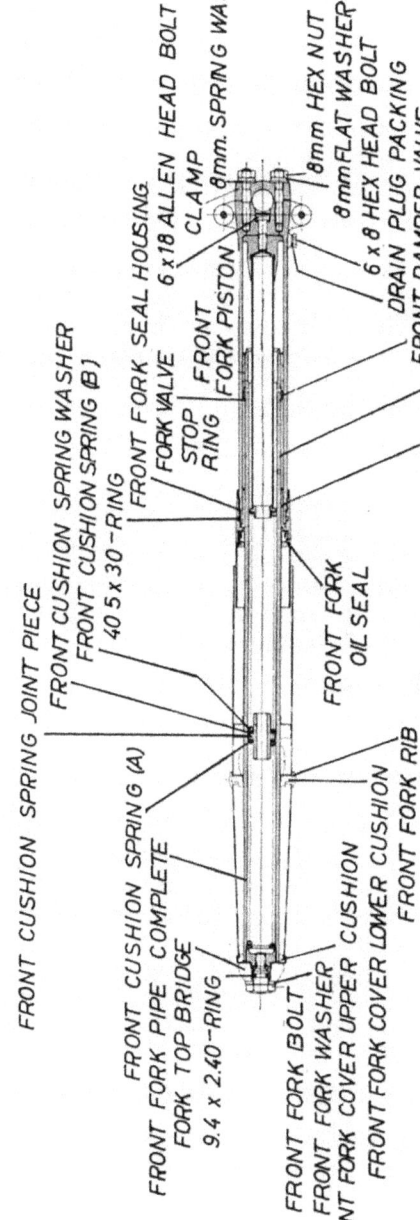

Fig. 41. This type of fork leg is basic to the entire range of machines fitted with telescopic front forks—the 160, 175, sports 250 and 305, and 450 c.c. motor-cycles

Remove the circlip from the damper piston and take off the piston, the damper valve, the stop ring, the guide bush and the seal housing.

12 The seal housing holds a spring-type oil seal, secured on its upper side by a wire circlip. Unless this seal requires renewal there is no need to disturb it—or even to take the seal housing off the fork leg. Where the seal is thought to be damaged, remove the circlip and press the seal out, working from the lower end of the housing.

13 Reassembly is basically a reversal of the sequence. Note, however, that it is essential to clean all parts thoroughly with methylated spirits and to allow them to dry. Do not use fluffy rag, which might upset the action of the damping. And take especial care not to damage the lip of the oil seal when refitting the seal housing.

14 After refitting the fork legs, replenish the oil supply (230 c.c. of SAE 30 mineral oil in each leg) before replacing the top bolts and tightening the clamping bolts.

Steering Head Renovation

Poor steering may be due to maladjustment of the steering head. This is checked by removing the handlebars and the fork top bridge, and gently tightening the upper steering head cone until there is no perceptible up-and-down play, but so that the forks will swing easily from side to side under their own weight. If damaged bearings are suspected, strip the head for examination in the following way—

1 Detach the handlebars.
2 Remove the front wheel.
3 Detach the fork legs.
4 Remove the fork top bridge by detaching the steering damper lock spring, pulling out the damper, and undoing the two 8 mm pinch bolts on the bridge clamp and unscrewing the steering-head nut.
5 Take off the headlamp rim and free the upper end of the speedometer cable and the rev. counter drive.
6 Lift away the headlamp cowling.
7 Release the upper cone by unscrewing it, supporting the underside of the stem as you do so.
8 Lower the steering head stem and lower bridge carefully from the frame.
9 Examine the tracks, both upper and lower, for signs of wear and the bearing balls for pitting or cracking. If any parts are found to be damaged or worn, the entire assembly must be renewed. Never use new balls in a worn track, or a new track with old balls.
10 To reassemble, grease the tracks and the bearing balls. Replace the balls on the lower track on the stem and on the track in the top of the steering head, and gently insert the stem. Screw down the

upper cone and adjust as already described. Then replace the remaining parts in the same order as before.

Leading-link Forks

In general, follow the same sequence for fork removal as that outlined above. Where the forks are to be stripped, however, the procedure is substantially different. In design, the leading link front fork resembles the rear suspension on a smaller scale. All that is necessary, therefore, is to remove the wheel and to take out each link complete with the spring/damper unit. This is done, quite simply, by removing the link pivot bolts and the upper pivot bolts for the units, which will then come out of the pressed-steel fork blades.

The dampers themselves are sealed, and cannot be dismantled. However, the spring can be freed by holding the top collar of the unit securely in a vice and compressing it sufficiently for the lock washer to be slackened. That done, the top collar can be unscrewed and the spring and its associated parts (collar, buffer and anti-rattle sleeve) slipped off the damper. Reassembly is a simple reversal of the same procedure.

Rear Suspension Units

Here, again, the damper units cannot be dismantled. The most which can be done is to remove them from the machine and fit new ones. The springs *can* be separated—by compressing the units in a special clamp; removing the large split collets which hold the upper case; and withdrawing the spring. Note that the springs are of two-rate type, the upper coils being spaced further apart than the lower ones.

Rear Fork Removal

All Honda rear suspension forks are of somewhat similar design. After detaching the rear wheel and the suspension units, the pivot bolt which passes through the frame is undone and the fork—complete with bushes—is lifted away.

Where the bushes require renewal, due to wear, the old parts can be driven out by use of a long drift inserted from the opposite side of the member.

New bushes can be drawn into place by pulling them in with a long bolt. On this bolt place a washer slightly larger in diameter than the bush. Then add the bush, and slide the bolt through the rear fork member. On the other side fix another washer, and a nut. By tightening the nut you can pull the bush into the pivot. Repeat the procedure for the other bush.

BRAKES

For day-to-day maintenance, all that the brakes require is to be kept in adjustment. This involves nothing more complicated than screwing out the adjusters to compensate for wear. The object is to set the brakes so that they are just clear of their drums, yet operate with the minimum movement of the controls.

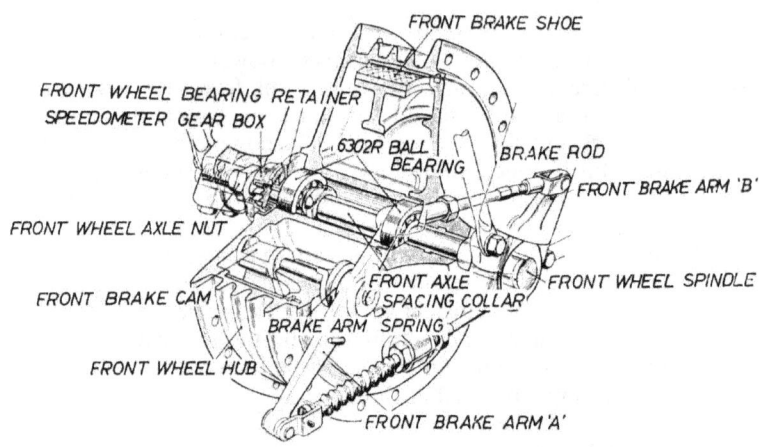

Fig. 42. The construction of a Honda twin-leading shoe front brake, as used on the sports models and the 450

When all the adjustment has been taken up—by this time the brake operating arm will form more than a right-angle with the cable when the

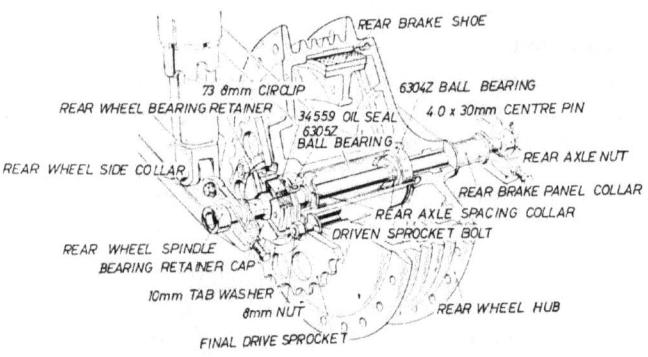

Fig. 43. The rear hub of the 450 in section. It contains a leading-and-trailing shoe brake, and again is typical of Honda practice

brake is applied—the shoes must be renewed. Do not re-line them yourself. Instead, use factory-lined replacement shoes.

The work involved is very simple. Remove the wheel, complete with

SUSPENSION AND BRAKES 85

the brake. Lift the brake plate away from the drum, and take it to the bench. You will see that the shoes are held together by springs. Note how these fit. Remove the pivot split pins and washers. Then ease the shoes sideways so that they disengage from their pivots. Take off the springs, fit them to the new shoes, and offer them up to the back-plate. You may find it easier to seat them on the pivots if you fit only one spring at this stage, and add the second one when the shoes are actually in place. Use new split pins on the pivots, and with twin leading shoe brakes check that the two cams synchronize with each other. If not, undo the lock-nuts on the interconnecting rod and vary its length until the same setting is obtained for both cams.

WHEEL BEARINGS

Save on the 450 c.c. model, where a special puller is required to remove the bearing retainer on the rear wheel, all Honda wheel bearings can be removed by driving them out with a drift inserted from the opposite side. New bearings are fitted by gentle tapping with a heavy hammer, using an interposed block of wood to prevent damage to the components.

APPENDIX: Facts and Figures

Data	C.92/95†	CB.92	C.72/77‡
Bore	44/49† mm	44 mm	54/60*** mm
Stroke	41 mm	41 mm	54 mm
Capacity	124/154†	124 c.c.	247/305***c. c.
C.R.	8·3:1	10:1	8·3:1
Output	11·5 b.h.p. at 9,500 r.p.m./16·5 b.h.p. at 10,000 r.p.m.†	15 b.h.p. at 10,500 r.p.m.	20 b.h.p .at 8,000 r.p.m.
Ignition timing (full advance)	40° b.t.d.c.	40° b.t.d.c.	40° b.t.d.c.
Ring gap (compression)	0·0059/0·014 in.	0·0059/0·014 in.	0·0059/0·014 in.
Ring gap (oil control rings)	0·0059/0·014 in.	0·0059/0·014 in.	0·0039/0·012 in.
Valve spring free length (outer)	1·137 in.		1·725 in.
Valve spring free length (inner)	1·189 in.		1·364 in.
Contact-breaker gap	0·012/0·020 in.		0·012/0·016 in.
Sparking plug gap	0·024/0·028 in.		0·027 in.
Tappet clearances		0·004 in. cold	
Main jet	90/95†	85	115/135‡
Slow-running jets	40	35	35
Throttle slide	Pw 18/520	Pw 18/2·5	Pw 22; Hov/520
Jet needle	Pw 18/24	Pw 18/24	Pw 22; Hov 24
Turns out, air adjuster screw	1/1½	1/1½	1/1½
Oil capacity		2·1 pints	2·7
Oil grade (winter)		20 S.A.E.	20
(summer)		30 S.A.E.	30
Petrol tank capacity	2·4 gal	2·8 gal	2·6 gal
Sparking plugs	C7H or C10H (10 mm × 12·7 mm reach) 1964 onwards: D9H (D8H during running in); D10 or D11; K.L.G. TW220 (TW100, town use). All 12 mm.		
Tyre pressure:			
front		25 p.s.i.	21 p.s.i.
rear		30 p.s.i.	28 p.s.i.
rear (pillion)		40 p.s.i.	40 p.s.i.
Bulbs:			
head		6 V 30/20 W	12 V 35/35 W
tail		6 V 3 W	12 V 4 W
stop		6 V 6 W	12 V 8 W
winker		6 V 8 W	12 V 10 W
neutral		6 V 2 W	12 V 3 W
parking			
winker or beam indicator			
speedo		6 V 3 W	12 V 3 W
Weight	264/273† lb	242 lb	356 lb
Length	76 in.	73½ in.	78·4 in.
Width	25½ in.	23½ in.	27.6 in.
Height	37·4 in.	36·4 in.	37·4 in.
Ground clearance	5·12 in.	5½ in.	5½ in.
Tyre sizes	3·00 × 16 in. front and rear	2·50 × 18 in. front 2·75 × 18 in. rear	3·25 × 16 in. front and rear

* Denotes data applicable to 305 c.c. Model C.B77 only.
† Denotes data applicable to 154 c.c. Model C.95 only
‡ Denotes data applicable to 305 c.c. Model C.77 only

	CB.72/77*	CB.160	CD.175A	CB.450
	54/60 mm* 54 mm 247/305 c.c.* 9·3:1 24/28½* b.h.p. at 9,000 r.p.m.	50 mm 41 mm 161 c.c. 9:1 16·5 b.h.p. at 10,000 r.p.m.	52 mm 41 mm 174 c.c. 9:1 17 b.h.p. at 10,500 r.p.m.	70 mm 57·8 mm 444 c.c. 8·5:1 43 b.h.p. at 8,500 r.p.m.
	45° b.t.d.c.	35° b.t.d.c.	40° b.t.d.c.	40° b.t.d.c.
	0·0059/0·013 in. 0·008/0·016 in.* 0·0039/0·012 in.	·0058/·0136 in.	·006/·018 in. ·006/·016 in.	·006/·014 in.
	1·707 in.	1·4 in.	1·25 in.	Torsion bars— not applicable
	1·477 in. 0·012/0·016 in. 0·027 in. (standard); 0·015 in. (racing)	1·1 in. 0·012/0·016 in. 0·024/0·028 in.	1·19 in. 0·012/0·016 in. 0·024/0·028 in.	0·012/0·016 in. 0·028/0·032 in.
	100/135* 35/42* 3/2*	0·004/0·006 in. cold 90 38 Varies	0·002 in. cold 98 40 31	0·001 in. cold 125 38 Not applicable
	22402/24231*	18331	2545	2·275
	1½/1¼* pints S.A.E. S.A.E. 3 gal C7HW or C10H C7HW (10 mm) B.C.C.TW220	1¼ 1·75 pints 10W 20W or 30 2·3 gal NGK D-8H or equivalent. NGK D-12H for high speeds	1⅛ 2·7 pints 10W 20 or 20W/or 30 2·5 gal NGK D-8HS or equivalent	⅞ 4·9 pints 10W 20 or 20W/or 30 3·5 gal NGK B-7E or equiva- lent. NGK B-9E for fast speeds
	24 p.s.i. 31 p.s.i.	26 p.s.i. 27 p.s.i. 31 p.s.i. (30 p.s.i. front)	26 p.s.i. 28½ p.s.i. 32 p.s.i.	26 p.s.i. 28 p.s.i. 30 p.s.i.
	12 V 35/30 W 12 V 4 W 12 V 7·5 W	12 V 30/30 W 12 V 25/8 W 12 V 3 W	6 V 35/35 W 6 V 5 W) 6V 18 W) 6 V 18 W 6 V 5 W 6V 4 W	12 V 35/30 W 12 V 25/8 W 12 V 10 W 12 V 3 W 12 V 3 W
	12 V 3 W 336/350* lb 79·7 in. 24·2 in. 39·4 in. 5·12 in. 2·75 × 18 in. front 3·00 × 18 in. rear	12 V 3 W 280 lb 76¾ in. 29⁵⁄₁₆ in. 39 in. 5¹¹⁄₁₆ in. 2·50 × 18 in. front 2·75 × 18 in. rear	6 V 5 W 6 V 3 W 260 lb 26·8 in. 73·6 in. 37·4 in. 5·3 in. 3·00 × 16 in. front and rear	12 V 3 W 12 V 3 W 412 lb 82·1 in. 30·7 in. 41·4 in. 5·3 in. 3·25 × 18 in. front 3·50 × 18 in. rear

NOTES

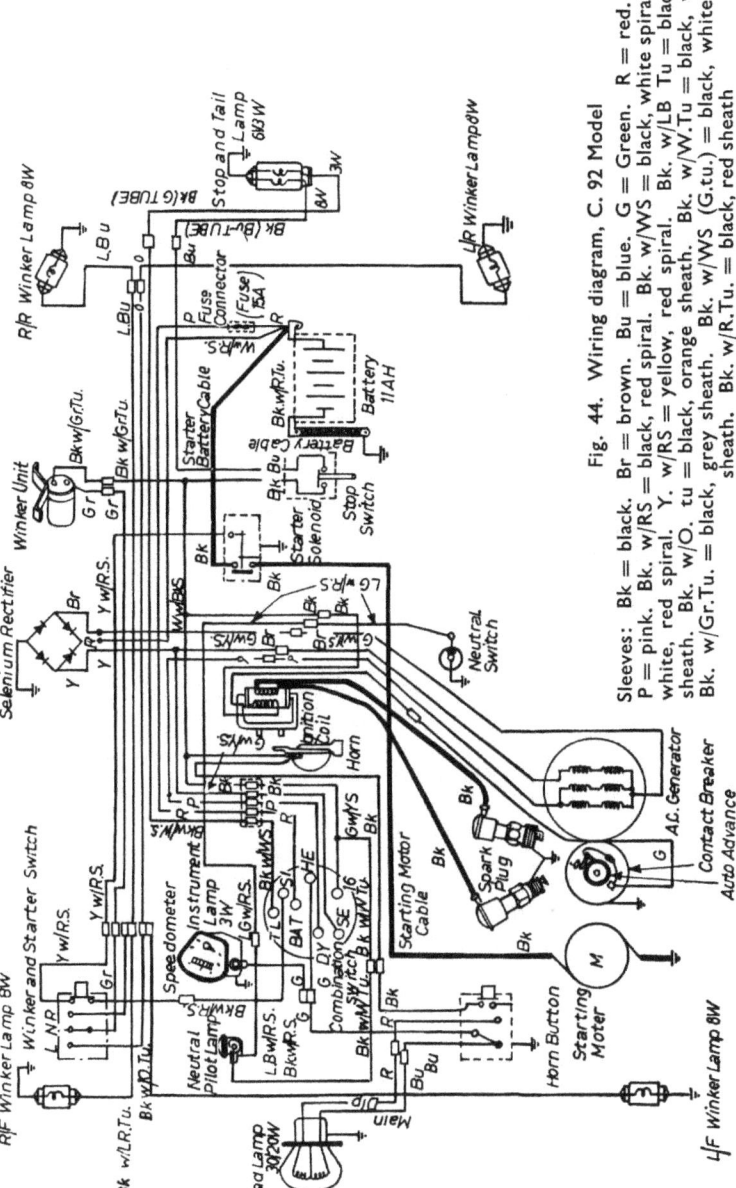

Fig. 44. Wiring diagram, C. 92 Model

Sleeves: Bk = black. Br = brown. Bu = blue. G = Green. R = red. Y = yellow. P = pink. Bk. w/RS = black, red spiral. Bk. w/WS = black, white spiral. W w/RS = white, red spiral. Y. w/RS = yellow, red spiral. Bk. w/LB Tu = black, light blue sheath. Bk. w/O. tu = black, orange sheath. Bk. w/W.Tu = black, white sheath. Bk. w/Gr.Tu. = black, grey sheath. Bk. w/WS (G.tu.) = black, white spiral, green sheath. Bk. w/R.Tu. = black, red spiral, red sheath

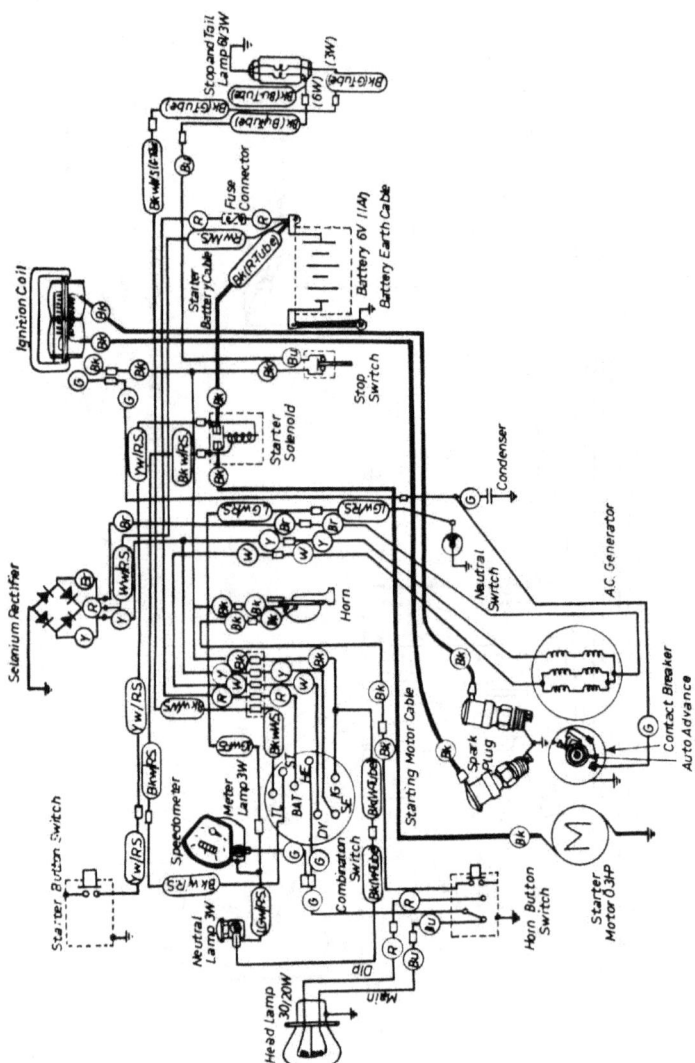

Fig. 45. Wiring diagram, CB. 92 Model

For abbreviations see Fig. 44—wiring diagram for Model C.92 twin

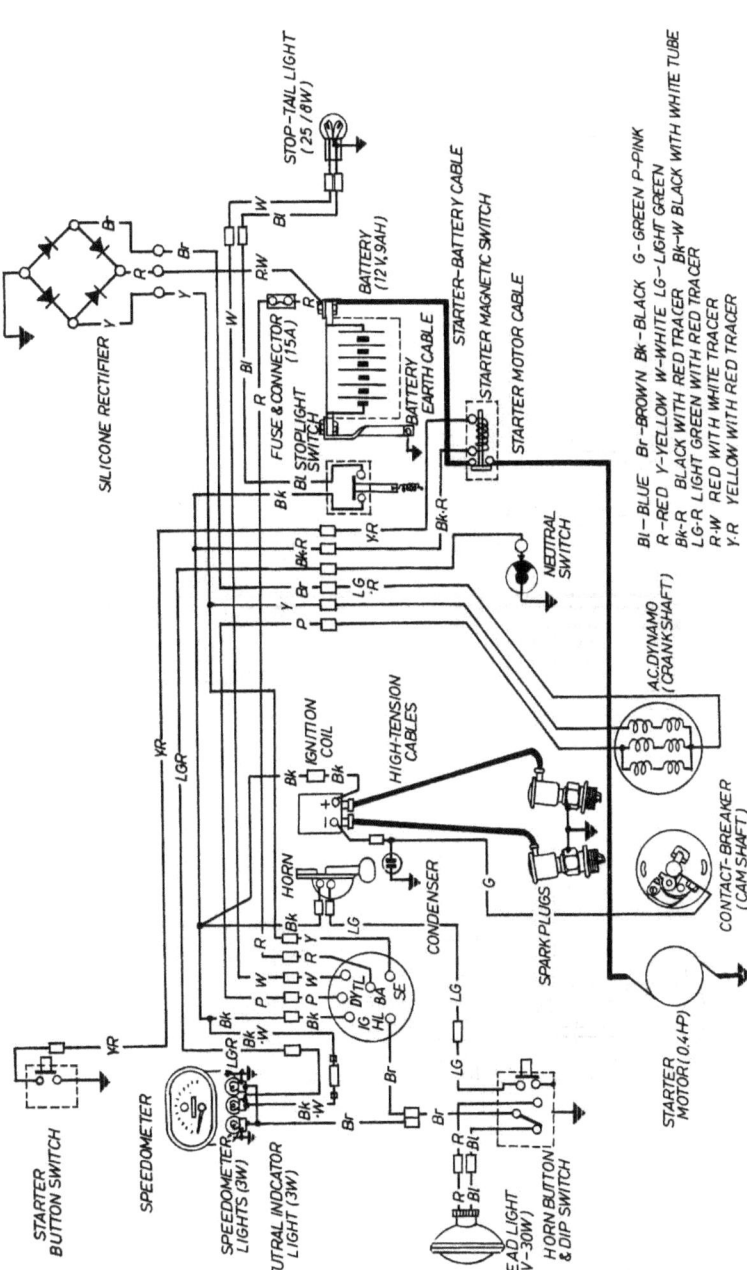

Fig. 46. Wiring diagram, 160 c.c. Model

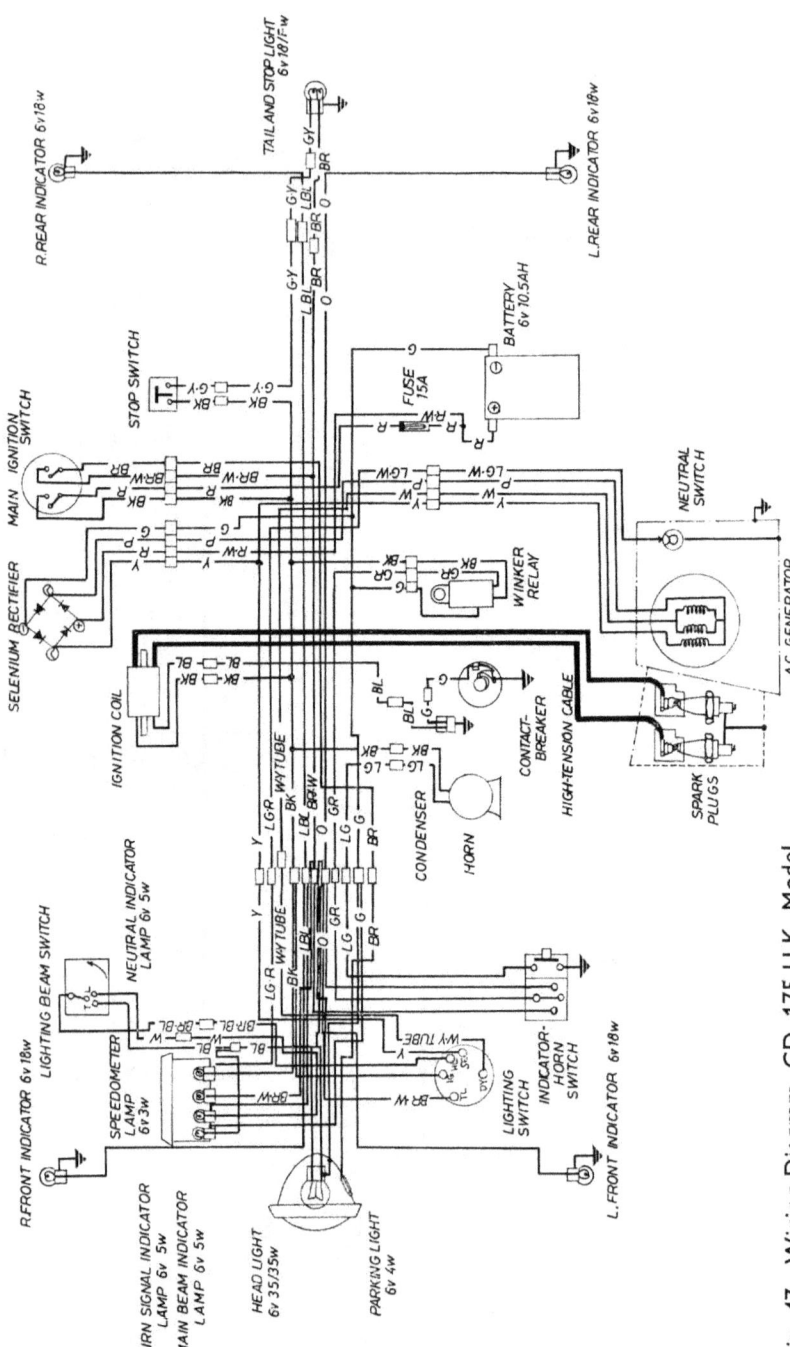

Fig. 47. Wiring Diagram, CD. 175 U.K. Model

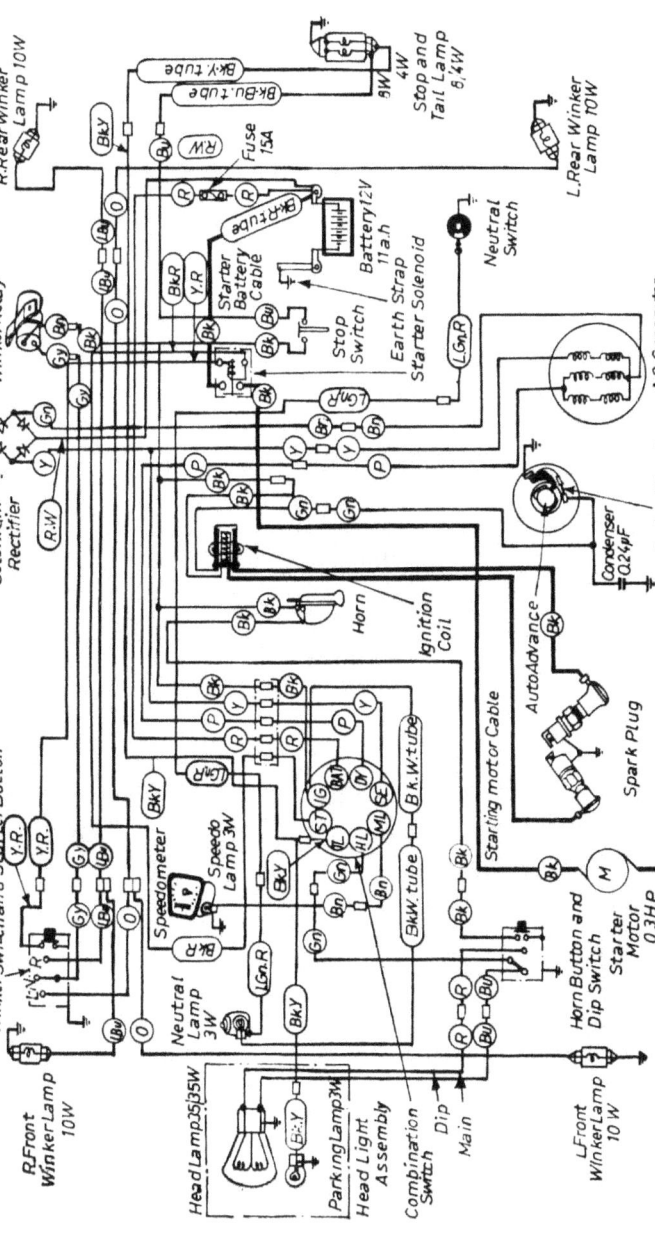

Fig. 48. Wiring diagram, C. 72 and C. 77 Models

Sleeves: Gy = grey. Bu = blue. Bk = black. Bn = brown. Gn = green. O = orange. W = white. Y = yellow. P = pink. L.Gn = light green. L.Bu = light blue. Bk.R = black/red. Bk.Y = black/yellow. R.W. = red/white. Y.R. = yellow/red. L.Gn.R. = light green/red. Bk.Y. tube = black, yellow sheath. Bk.Bu tube = black, blue sheath. Bk R. tube = black, red sheath. Bk W. tube = black, white sheath

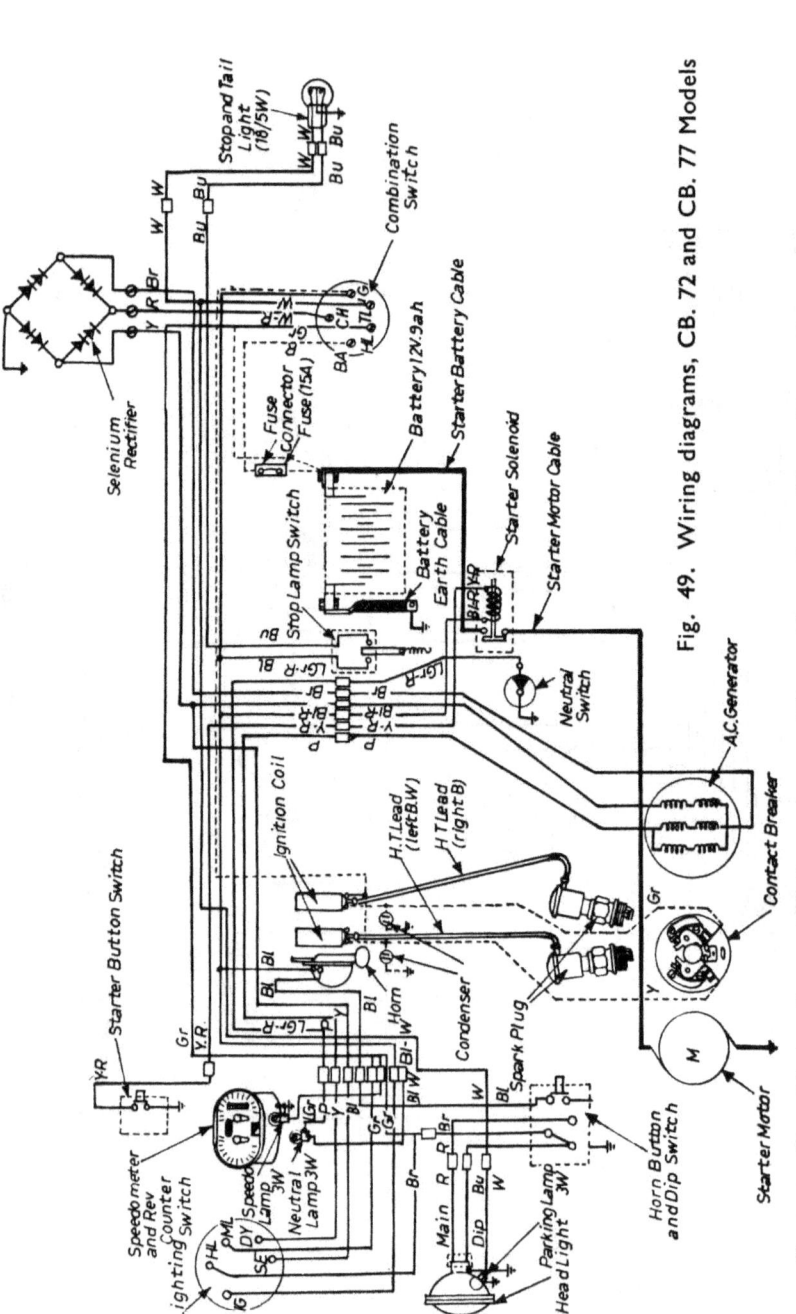

Fig. 49. Wiring diagrams, CB. 72 and CB. 77 Models

Sleeves: Bl = black. R = red. Gr = green. W = white. Bu = blue. Y = yellow. Br = brown. P = pink. L.Gr = light green. Bl & Rr = black/red. Y & R = yellow/red. L.Gr & R = light green/red. W & R = white/red. Bl & W = black/white. Solid lines, harness "B." Dotted lines, harness "A."

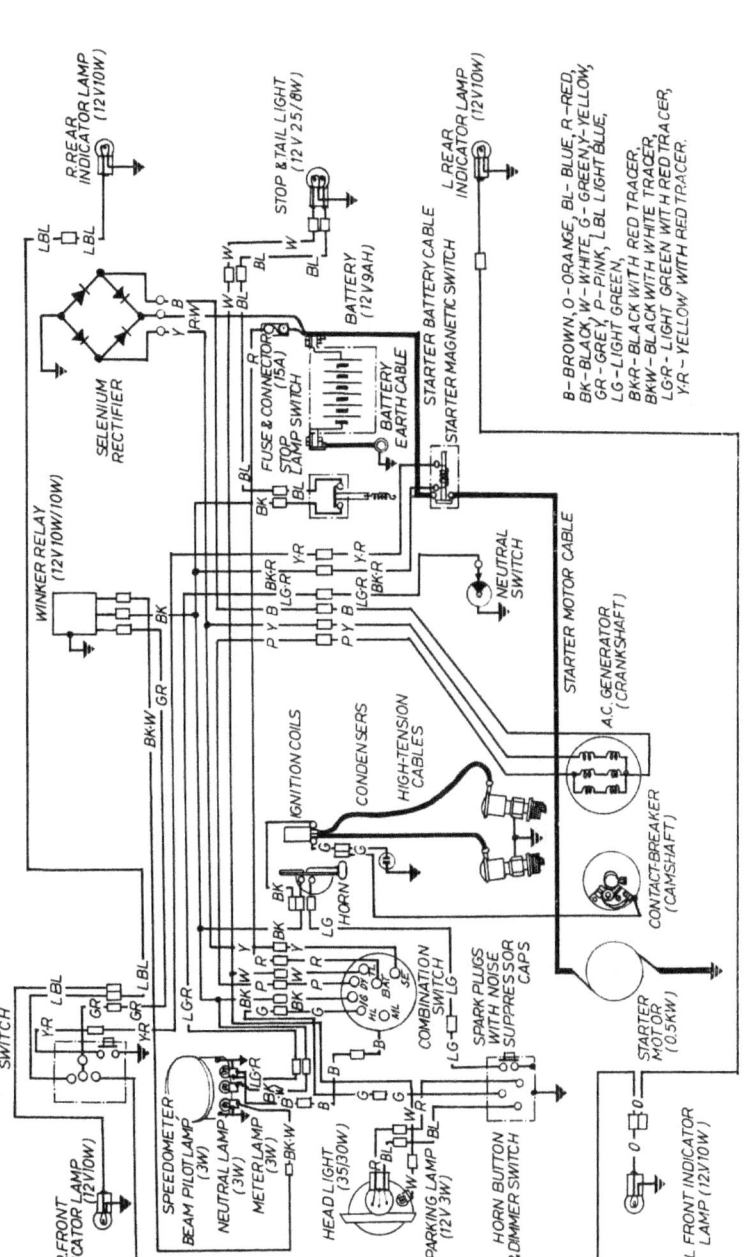

Fig. 50. Wiring Diagram, 450 c.c. Model, General Export Type

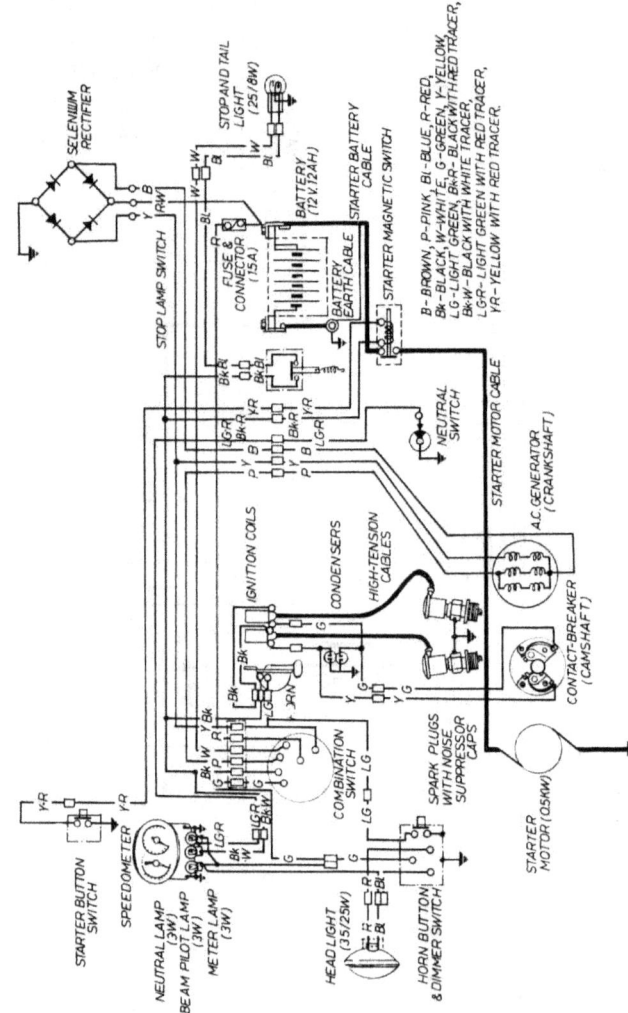

Fig. 51. Wiring Diagram, 450 c.c. Model, U.K. Type

Index

Adjustments, data, *see* Appendix, 86, 87; also C.72, CB.72, C.77, CB.77, C.92, CB.92, CB.160, CB.450, CD.175

Bolts, freeing, 9
Brakes, adjusting, 83, 84
  leading and trailing shoe, 84
  shoe renewal, 84, 85
  two leading shoe, 84

Carburettor, exploded, 75
C.72, C.77
  clutch, re-assembly, 62
  clutch, removal, 62
  data, maintenance, 86, 87
  engine, removal, 58
  gearbox, stripping, 63
  head nuts, tightening sequence, 60
  head, re-assembly, 60
  head, removal, 60
  re-timing, 60
  valve gear, removal, 60
CB.72, CB.77
  cam chain tensioner, 59
  carburettor, exploded, 76
  clutch, exploded, 61
  clutch, re-assembly, 62
  clutch, removal, 62
  data, maintenance, 86, 87
  engine, removal, 58, 59, 60
  gearbox, stripping, 63
  head nuts, tightening sequence, 60
  head, re-assembly, 74
  head, removal, 74
  re-timing, 60
  valve gear, removal, 60
C.92, CB.92
  carburettor, exploded, 74
  clutch, exploded, 43

C.92, CB.92 (*contd.*)—
  clutch, re-assembly, 42
  clutch, removal, 42
  data, maintenance, 86, 87
  engine, removal, 39
  gearbox, stripping, 42, 44, 45
  head, re-fitting, 41
  head, removal, 40
  oil pump, exploded, 44
  re-timing, 41
  valve gear, removal, 41
CB.160
  clutch, removal, 51
  crankcase, splitting, 51, 52
  cylinder, removal, 50
  data, maintenance, 86, 87
  engine, re-fitting, 47
  engine, removal, 46
  generator, 49
  head, removal, 47, 48
  head, replacing, 48
  ignition timing, 49
  oil pump, checking, 51
  oil pump, removal, 48
  piston rings, gapping, 50
  piston rings, removal, 50
  re-timing, 48, 49
  ring grooves, clearance, 50
CB.450
  advance/retard mechanism, 66
  cam chain adjuster, 70
  cam chain tensioner, 68
  clutch, removal, 69, 70
  crankcase, splitting, 70, 72
  cylinder, removal, 69
  data, maintenance, 86, 87
  engine, removal, 64
  head, re-assembly, 66, 67
  head, removal, 65, 66
  oil pump, checking, 70

INDEX

CB.450 (*contd.*)—
  oil pump, exploded, 67
  re-timing, 68
  starter, sectioned, 73
  timing marks, 65
  valve tappet adjustment, 11, 12, 13, 69
CD.175
  crankcase, splitting, 55, 56, 57
  cylinder, removal, 54, 55
  data, maintenance, 86, 87
  engine, re-assembly, 57
  engine, removal, 53, 54
  head, removal, 54
  kickstarter, removal, 57
  re-timing, 55
Cam chain tensioner, 38
Carburettor—
  constant vacuum,
    adjusters, 78
    adjustment, 79
    cross section, 78
    operation, 77, 79
  needle jet type, 18
  high-speed adjustment, 77
  mid-speed adjustment, 77
  slow running adjustment, 73
Chain—
  lubrication, 19, 20
  repairing, 20
  wear test, 19
Clutch—
  adjustment, 2, 3
  slip, 26, 27
Contact-breaker—
  diagram, 24
  gap, 86, 87
  testing, 24
Cylinder head, decarbonizing, 37 (*see also specific models*)

Decarbonizing, general, 35, 36, 37, 38

Electrics, waterlogged, 25
Engine failure, mechanical, 25

Fork, rear, removal, 83
Forks—
  leading link,
    removal, 83
    stripping, 83

Forks (*contd.*)—
  telescopic,
    cross-section, 81
    dismantling, 80, 82

Head nuts, tightening, 36 (*see also specific models*)

Jets, cleaning, 22

Lighting, fault tracing, 27, 28
Lubrication, 18, 19

Maintenance data, 86, 87

Oil changes, 4, 5, 6
Oil filter, 14, 15, 16, 17
  cleaning, 6
Oils, recommended, 86, 87

Piston crowns, polishing, 37
  rings, broken, 25
  rings, clearances, 86, 87
Plug caps, 17
  leads, 17, 23
Plugs, faults, 22, 23, 24
  gaps, 86, 87
  general, 14, 15, 16
  heat range, 23
  recommended, 86, 87

Sparking plugs, *see* Plugs
Starter motor—
  freewheel, 62
  general, 17, 18, 61
Steering head, renovation, 82, 83
Sump, drain plug, 6
Suspension legs, rear, stripping, 83

Tappets—
  adjustments, 11, 12, 13, 14, 86, 87
  (also *see* specific models)
  tight, 25
Task systems, 3, 4
Tools, 7, 8, 9, 10
Trouble tracer, 29, 30, 31, 32, 33, 34
Trouble tracing, methodical, 21, 22
Tyre pressures, 86, 87

Valve gear, arrangement, 26
  seats, checking, 38

INDEX

Valves—
  grinding-in, 37, 38
  re-cutting, 37

Wheel bearings, renewal, 85
Wiring diagram—
  C.72, C.77 models, 93
  C.92 model, 89

Wiring diagram (*contd.*)—
  CB.72, CB.77 models, 94
  CB.92 model, 90
  CB.160 model, 91
  CB.450 Export model, 95
  CB.450 U.K. model, 96
  CD.175 model, 92
Wiring, testing, 24

ARE YOU:
INTERESTED IN EUROPEAN, IMPORT & EXOTIC AUTOMOBILES?

DO YOU:
DO YOUR OWN MAINTENANCE?

If you answered yes to either of these questions, then you should check out our automobile books and manuals. We have included a sample listing of some of our featured marques. However, for complete details and the most up-to-date information, please visit our website.

—— www.VelocePress.com ——

The fastest growing specialist USA publisher of niche market automotive books and manuals.

All VelocePress titles are available through your local independent bookseller, Amazon.com or direct from VelocePress. Wholesale customers may also purchase direct or from the Ingram Book Group.

AUTOBOOKS WORKSHOP MANUALS

ALFA ROMEO GIULIA 1300, 1600, 1750, 2000 1962-1978 WSM
AUSTIN HEALEY SPRITE, MG MIDGET 1958-1980 WSM
BMW 1600 1966-1973 WSM
BMW 2000 & 2002 1966-1976 WSM
BMW 2500, 2800, 3.0 & 3.3 1968-1977 WSM
BMW 316, 320, 320i 1975-1977 WSM
BMW 518, 520, 520i 1973-1981 WSM
FIAT 1100, 1100D, 1100R & 1200 1957-1969 WSM
FIAT 124 1966-1974 WSM
FIAT 124 SPORT 1966-1975 WSM
FIAT 125 & 125 SPECIAL 1967-1973 WSM
FIAT 126, 126L, 126 DV, 126/650 & 126/650 DV 1972-1982 WSM
FIAT 127 SALOON, SPECIAL & SPORT, 900, 1050 1971-1981 WSM
FIAT 128 1969-1982 WSM
FIAT 1300, 1500 1961-1967 WSM
FIAT 131 MIRAFIORI 1975-1982 WSM
FIAT 132 1972-1982 WSM
FIAT 500 1957-1973 WSM
FIAT 600, 600D & MULTIPLA 1955-1969 WSM
FIAT 850 1964-1972 WSM
JAGUAR E-TYPE 1961-1972 WSM
JAGUAR MK 1, 2 1955-1969 WSM
JAGUAR S TYPE, 420 1963-1968 WSM
JAGUAR XK 120, 140, 150 MK 7, 8, 9 1948-1961 WSM
LAND ROVER 1, 2 1948-1961 WSM
MERCEDES-BENZ 190 1959-1968 WSM
MERCEDES-BENZ 220/8 1968-1972 WSM
MERCEDES-BENZ 220B 1959-1965 WSM
MERCEDES-BENZ 230 1963-1968 WSM
MERCEDES-BENZ 250 1968-1972 WSM
MERCEDES-BENZ 280 1968-1972 WSM
MG MIDGET TA-TF 1936-1955 WSM
MINI 1959-1980 WSM
MORRIS MINOR 1952-1971 WSM
PEUGEOT 404 1960-1975 WSM
PORSCHE 911 1964-1973 WSM
PORSCHE 911 1970-1977 WSM
RENAULT 16 1965-1979 WSM
RENAULT 8, 10, 1100 1962-1971 WSM
ROVER 3500, 3500S 1968-1976 WSM
SUNBEAM RAPIER, ALPINE 1955-1965 WSM
TRIUMPH SPITFIRE, GT6, VITESSE 1962-1968 WSM
TRIUMPH TR2, TR3, TR3A 1952-1962 WSM
TRIUMPH TR4, TR4A 1961-1967 WSM
VOLKSWAGEN BEETLE 1968-1977 WSM

BROOKLANDS BOOKS & ROAD TEST PORTFOLIOS (RTP)

AC CARS 1904-2009
ALFA ROMEO 1920-1933 ROAD TEST PORTFOLIO
ALFA ROMEO 1934-1940 ROAD TEST PORTFOLIO
BRABHAM RALT HONDA THE RON TAURANAC STORY
BUGATTI TYPE 10 TO TYPE 40 ROAD TEST PORTFOLIO
BUGATTI TYPE 10 TO TYPE 251 ROAD TEST PORTFOLIO
BUGATTI TYPE 41 TO TYPE 55 ROAD TEST PORTFOLIO
BUGATTI TYPE 57 TO TYPE 251 ROAD TEST PORTFOLIO
DELAHAYE ROAD TEST PORTFOLIO
FERRARI ROAD CARS 1946-1956 ROAD TEST PORTFOLIO
FIAT 500 1936-1972 ROAD TEST PORTFOLIO
FIAT DINO ROAD TEST PORTFOLIO
HISPANO SUIZA ROAD TEST PORTFOLIO
HONDA ST1100/ST1300 PAN EUROPEAN 1990-2002 RTP
JAGUAR MK1 & MK2 ROAD TEST PORTFOLIO
LOTUS CORTINA ROAD TEST PORTFOLIO
MV AGUSTA F4 750 & 1000 1997-2007 ROAD TEST PORTFOLIO
TATRA CARS ROAD TEST PORTFOLIO

VELOCEPRESS AUTOMOBILE BOOKS & MANUALS

ABARTH BUYERS GUIDE
AUSTIN-HEALEY 6-CYLINDER WSM
BMW 600 LIMOUSINE FACTORY WSM
BMW 600 LIMOUSINE OWNERS HAND BOOK & SERVICE MANUAL
BMW ISETTA FACTORY WSM
BOOK OF THE CARRERA PANAMERICANA - MEXICAN ROAD RACE
COMPLETE CATALOG OF JAPANESE MOTOR VEHICLES
DIALED IN - THE JAN OPPERMAN STORY
FERRARI 250/GT SERVICE AND MAINTENANCE
FERRARI 308 SERIES BUYER'S AND OWNER'S GUIDE
FERRARI BERLINETTA LUSSO
FERRARI BROCHURES AND SALES LITERATURE 1946-1967
FERRARI BROCHURES AND SALES LITERATURE 1968-1989
FERRARI GUIDE TO PERFORMANCE
FERRARI OPP, MAINTENANCE & SERVICE H/BOOKS 1948-1963
FERRARI OWNER'S HANDBOOK
FERRARI SERIAL NUMBERS PART I - ODD NUMBERS TO 21399
FERRARI SERIAL NUMBERS PART II - EVEN NUMBERS TO 1050
FERRARI SPYDER CALIFORNIA
FERRARI TUNING TIPS & MAINTENANCE TECHNIQUES
HOW TO BUILD A FIBERGLASS CAR
HOW TO BUILD A RACING CAR
IF HEMINGWAY HAD WRITTEN A RACING NOVEL
JAGUAR E-TYPE 3.8 & 4.2 WSM
LE MANS 24 (THE BOOK THAT THE FILM WAS BASED ON)
MASERATI BROCHURES AND SALES LITERATURE
MASERATI OWNER'S HANDBOOK
METROPOLITAN FACTORY WSM
MGA & MGB OWNERS HANDBOOK & WSM
OBERT'S FIAT GUIDE
PERFORMANCE TUNING THE SUNBEAM TIGER
PORSCHE 356 1948-1965 WSM
PORSCHE 912 WSM
SOUPING THE VOLKSWAGEN
TRIUMPH TR2, TR3, TR4 1953-1965 WSM
VEDA ORR'S NEW REVISED HOT ROD PICTORIAL
VOLKSWAGEN TRANSPORTER, TRUCKS, STATION WAGONS WSM
VOLVO 1944-1968 ALL MODELS WSM

VELOCEPRESS MOTORCYCLE BOOKS & MANUALS

AJS SINGLES 1955-65 350cc & 500cc (BOOK OF)
ARIEL 1939-1960 4 STROKE SINGLES (BOOK OF)
ARIEL LEADER & ARROW 1958-1964 (BOOK OF)
ARIEL MOTORCYCLES 1933-1951 WSM
ARIEL PREWAR MODELS 1932-1939 (BOOK OF)
BMW M/CYCLES R26 R27 (1956-1967) FACTORY WSM
BMW M/CYCLES R50 R50S R60 R69S (1955-1969) FACTORY WSM
BSA BANTAM (BOOK OF)
BSA ALL FOUR-STROKE SINGLES & V-TWINS 1936-1952 (BOOK OF)
BSA OHV & SV SINGLES - 250cc 1954-1970 (BOOK OF)
BSA OHV & SV SINGLES 1945-54 250-600cc (BOOK OF)
BSA OHV SINGLES 350 & 500cc 1955-1967 (BOOK OF)
BSA PRE-WAR MODELS TO 1939 (BOOK OF)
BSA TWINS 1948-1962 (BOOK OF)
BSA TWINS 1962-1969 (SECOND BOOK OF)
DOUGLAS PRE-WAR ALL MODELS 1929-1939 (BOOK OF)
DOUGLAS POST-WAR ALL MODELS 1948-1957 FACTORY WSM
DUCATI 160cc, 250cc, & 350cc OHC MODELS FACTORY WSM
HONDA 50 ALL MODELS UP TO 1970 INC MONKEY & TRAIL (BOOK OF)
HONDA 90 ALL MODELS UP TO 1966 (BOOK OF)
HONDA MOTORCYCLES 125-150 TWINS C/CS/CB/CA WSM
HONDA MOTORCYCLES 250-305 TWINS C/CS/CB WSM
HONDA MOTORCYCLES C100 SUPER CUB WSM
HONDA MOTORCYCLES C110 SPORT CUB 1962-1969 WSM
HONDA TWINS & SINGLES 50cc TO 305cc 1960-1966 (BOOK OF)
HONDA TWINS ALL MODELS 125cc THRU 450cc UP TO 1968 (BOOK OF)
LAMBRETTA ALL 125 & 150cc MODELS 1947-1957 (BOOK OF)
LAMBRETTA LI & TV MODELS 1957-1970 (SECOND BOOK OF)
MATCHLESS 350 & 500cc SINGLES 1945-1956 (BOOK OF)
MATCHLESS 350 & 500cc SINGLES 1955-1966 (BOOK OF)
NORTON 1938-1956 (BOOK OF)
NORTON DOMINATOR TWINS 1955-1965 (BOOK OF)
NORTON MOTORCYCLES 1957-1970 FACTORY WSM
NORTON PREWAR MODELS 1932-1939 (BOOK OF)
ROYAL ENFIELD 736cc INTERCEPTOR FACTORY WSM
ROYAL ENFIELD 250cc & 350cc SINGLES 1958-1970 (SECOND BOOK OF)
SUZUKI 50cc & 80cc UP TO 1966 (BOOK OF)
SUZUKI T10 1963-1967 FACTORY WSM
SUZUKI T20 & T200 1965-1969 FACTORY WSM
TRIUMPH PRE-WAR MOTORCYCLE 1935-1939 (BOOK OF)
TRIUMPH MOTORCYCLES 1937-1951 WSM
TRIUMPH MOTORCYCLES 1945-1955 FACTORY WSM
TRIUMPH TWINS 1956-1969 (BOOK OF)
VELOCETTE ALL SINGLES & TWINS 1925-1970 (BOOK OF)
VESPA 1951-1961 (BOOK OF)
VINCENT MOTORCYCLES 1935-1955 WSM

www.VelocePress.com

www.ingramcontent.com/pod-product-compliance
Lightning Source LLC
Chambersburg PA
CBHW070600170426
43201CB00012B/1884